"The Boss of the Whole School"

"The Boss of the Whole School"

Effective Leadership in Action

Elizabeth A. Hebert

FOREWORD BY

Richard H. Ackerman

Teachers College
Columbia University
New York and London

Published by Teachers College Press, 1234 Amsterdam Avenue, New York, NY 10027

A substantial portion of Chapter 4 previously appeared in *Phi Delta Kappan*. It is included in this work with their permission: E. A. Hebert, "Rugtime for Teachers: Reinventing the Faculty Meeting," *Phi Delta Kappan*, 1999, *81*(3), 219–222.

Library of Congress Cataloging-in-Publication Data

Hebert, Elizabeth A. (Elizabeth Ann), 1950–
    The boss of the whole school : effective leadership in action / Elizabeth A. Hebert.
       p. cm.
    Includes bibliographical references and index.
    Contents: Contents: Imagine being a principal — Leading a school and managing a school: what's the difference? — Creating traditions: how a school gains an identity — Rugtime for teachers: reinventing the faculty meeting and mentoring good ideas — Hire teachers as if your professional life depends on it: it does — "He stole my snow": moral dimensions of leadership on the playground — "Who'd you get?": the yearly ritual of classroom placement — Administrative aloneness: the darker side of the principalship — Imagine not being a principal: passing the baton.
    ISBN-13: 978-0-8077-4697-4 (cloth : alk. paper)
    ISBN-13: 978-0-8077-4696-7 (pbk. : alk. paper)
    ISBN-10: 0-8077-4697-5 (cloth : alk. paper)
    ISBN-10: 0-8077-4696-7 (pbk. : alk. paper)
    1. School principals—United States. 2. Educational leadership—United States.
    3. School management and organization—United States. I. Title.

LB2831.92.H43 2006
                                                                    2005046709

ISBN-13:   ISBN-10:
978-0-8077-4696-7 (paper)   0-8077-4696-7 (paper)
978-0-8077-4697-4 (cloth)   0-8077-4697-5 (cloth)

Printed on acid-free paper

Manufactured in the United States of America

13 12 11 10 09 08 07 06   8 7 6 5 4 3 2 1

Contents

Foreword

There are many books published today on the subject of the principalship. Those with a vested interest in school leadership have available in this literature a remarkable array of approaches to the task. However, the meaning of the principal's work seems more varied, wide-ranging, and complex than ever. Elizabeth Hebert's *"The Boss of the Whole School,"* stands out. It reckons honestly and beautifully with an essential attribute of leadership work: that the practice is learnable, and worth learning.

Elizabeth Hebert accomplishes in this book precisely what she asks novice and veteran principals to do. She is able to get on the balcony and be on the floor at the same time. This capacity for greeting principalship work with a set of shifting perspectives—linking the dailyness of the principal's life to the larger potential for leadership—is refreshing and rewarding. It is the kind of flexibility we need in principals today—seeing anew what really matters in the work. What shines through this account for me is a leadership imagination and spirit I have yearned to find in a book on the principalship. It leaves me, as I believe it will leave you, with the sense that the principalship in theory and practice can be elegantly conceived and gracefully done.

"The Boss of the Whole School" captures things about the principalship that are not always easily and readily available to practitioners. The dilemmas and descriptions carry the themes of the book in a hopeful, enthusiastic, and inquiring way. The organizing logic for the book is elegantly simple, focusing on a principal's relationships with teachers, students, and herself. The topics are eminently practical, examining issues that range from the teacher hiring process to the placement of students. However, Elizabeth Hebert treats these age-old principal dilemmas with space and openness and lets these stories carry her learnings well. While the book is filled with practical wisdom and humble "how-tos," gleaned from a stunning twenty-one year career, the approach here is not time-locked. There are no finished realities here. The language reflects the joys and frustrations of principalship life on the ground, revealing a comforting sense of the familiar while sharing many things new and true.

Also important, this book is about a real and remarkable person, Elizabeth Hebert, stepping back into the daily devotion and challenges of being a public school principal. As such, it is about a person willing to be present to her leadership self-being formed in what is told. And so, the act of telling for Elizabeth Hebert *and* the reader, is a dual affirmation.

What the stories in this book teach is the sheer delight—perhaps the child's delight from which the title of the book is inspired—of being totally within one's element, of identifying fully with one's work and seeing it as an expression of one's self. "*The Boss of the Whole School*" is an invitation to look deeply and compassionately at the leadership life at hand, and to learn what is essential there. Such passion the book inspires us to feel can be cultivated in the life of the principal and the work of the principalship.

RICHARD H. ACKERMAN

1

Imagine Being a Principal

Do you want to be a principal? Why? What do you know about that job? Maybe you're thinking about other principals you've known or observed. You'll probably want to replicate what worked well for them, in your opinion, and avoid or at least ameliorate problems they encountered. But there's more to the principal's job than copying what others have done. Are you hoping that there's a job manual that you can study and follow explicitly? Unfortunately, there isn't. If you do become a principal, I have this advice for you: for the most part, your leadership will be formed by who you are—your own life experiences, your temperament, and your judgment. These unchangeables will shape your authority, be embedded in the many decisions you'll make, and be recognized as the image of your leadership. Who you are and how you think will be of great interest to those you lead, so take some time to imagine being a principal and consider your capacity for this important and perplexing leadership role.

TEMPTATION. I was determined to resist it. Comfortable with the development of my career so far, a profound and life-altering change of job was the furthest thing from my mind. Nevertheless, I sat nervously in the superintendent's outer office waiting for him to return from a meeting. It was a rainy Tuesday afternoon, July 3, 1984. I had been invited to interview for the principalship of Crow Island Elementary School in Winnetka, Illinois. I had just completed my doctorate in administration and supervision, and so I was seeking any kind of interviewing experience. This meeting would fill that bill except that I certainly was not looking for a principalship—at least, not at first.

As a teacher, I had worked under several different principals. I thought I knew what principals did, and I couldn't imagine myself in that role. More recently, as a supervisor of special education programs in public elementary schools, I had observed many principals—men mostly—weighted down with enormous responsibilities. I overheard them meeting with scores of angry parents or in deep conversation with their secretaries about classroom furniture orders. I saw them stand guard as a symbol of safety in the chaotic morning hallways. I listened to these principals making announcements on the school intercom each morning, affirming their leadership with weather reports and reminders of special schedules so that busy teachers could manage their day. I watched them fly from one end of the building to the other, responding to a teacher's intercom buzz to retrieve a recalcitrant youth from a classroom and talk to him about respect and the consequences of bad behavior. I observed them wave off the buses at the end of the day with that unmistakable intent expression of responsibility on their faces, and then slowly walk back into the building with heads down, as if examining the sidewalk. Mostly, though, from the security of my perch as a consulting supervisor, I remember being keenly aware of how teachers regard their principal.

WHAT TEACHERS THINK ABOUT A PRINCIPAL

An undercurrent of wariness was ever-present when I noticed the teachers' interactions with their principal. When I was a teacher, I'm sure I, too, had internalized that attitude, but I was not consciously aware of it. However, as a consultant and observer of the teacher/principal relationship, it was not difficult to see. I would often overhear a teacher engaging a principal in a friendly conversation, and these daily principal–teacher interactions seemed pleasant enough: "How was your weekend?" "Oh, the usual." "Brian still working on those college applications? Same with our Kevin—he may never leave us!" They both laugh and shake their heads, stepping out of their respective work roles, acknowledging their common role of parent. Still, there was a subtle difference in tone. I know how teachers talk to teachers. These teachers spoke differently to their principal. Did it sound more formal? Was it just a few decibels louder, to be sure that any passing teacher would overhear the exchange? I wondered if the intent of this raised volume was to subtly reinforce allegiance to the teachers' code of "I'm not telling any secrets to this principal—you can trust me."

This wasn't the only interpersonal anomaly. Surely these principals must notice the not-so-subtle shift in conversation and demeanor when they wandered into the teachers' lounge. Sometimes I winced when I witnessed this visibly excluding behavior. But I never said anything. I was just glad that the teachers continued their gossip when I was in the room, affirming, to my relief, that I caused no similar need for them to cope with who I was or what I represented.

There were other behaviors—obvious ones—that amplified how teachers regarded the principal. I noted teachers rolling their eyes at their principal's announcements at faculty meetings, criticizing their principal's memos and requests for teacher ideas, attributing sinister motivations to their principal's comments, and vacating the building for lunch at noon on staff development days without even considering inviting their principal to join them. I never once asked why.

I worked in many different school buildings, and so I soon realized the uncanny pervasiveness of this conduct—that "certain something" that separated the teachers from the principal, whether that principal was a tyrant or the most gracious and accessible school leader. To varying degrees, it was always present. All these unvenerated men and women had but one thing in common—they were the principal. The habitual teacher demeanor toward them wasn't about the person who held that role; it was about the role that held that person—that administrative "DNA" that predominates personhood during a principal's tenure.

Still, there I was, seated in that outer office on that rainy Tuesday afternoon, waiting to interview for a principalship, a job I viewed with understandable skepticism, if not dislike, for what seemed to be its enormous responsibilities and substantially unrewarding nature. I reminded myself that I was here for the interview—not the job. I had been recommended for this post by another superintendent who, having gotten to know my work as a special education supervisor, thought I might be a good principal. I was confident that I knew what a principal's job entailed, and equally confident that I didn't want to be one. I was armed with resolve not to adjust my life to encompass that particular administrative duty. I composed some polite sentences in my mind that would conclude the interview.

More than 2 hours later, I left that superintendent's office having forgotten those sentences and having abandoned my resolve. I was hoping to be invited back for the next stage of the recruiting process. So much for resisting temptation.

THAT FIRST INTERVIEW

What changed my mind? The interview started easily and pleasantly. I was relieved about the conversational tone that was quickly established. The Winnetka Public Schools enjoy a long and significant record of excellence (Washburne & Marland, 1963), often alluded to in history of education courses, and we talked about some of the many highlights of that story. I kept waiting for this superintendent to tell me more specifics about the principal's job. But he didn't do that. Smart man. Instead, he maintained a conversational tone, gently probing about my life, my attitudes, my "me-ness." I had no idea what this had to do with being a principal of an elementary school—not a clue. So I went along responding courteously and enjoying the conversation.

Then he asked me an unusual question: "Can you be autonomous?" The question was unexpected. What did he mean? Weren't principals supposed to comply with central office procedures? Wasn't there some kind of manual that I was to study and follow explicitly? I considered the principals I knew. I would not describe them as autonomous; some were less beleaguered than others, but certainly none operated with what I thought of as self-determination. Autonomy to me implied self-direction, self-reliance. Someone who is autonomous initiates—doesn't wait to be told. An autonomous person goes beyond the known and creates new structures for knowing. Autonomy suggested independence.

CAN I BE AUTONOMOUS?

Well, could I be autonomous? I held a doctorate and credential in administration and supervision of schools. I was well versed in issues of school law, supervision of staff, community relations, curriculum development, school budgets, and crisis management. I got A's in all my coursework and I had been successful as a supervisor of special education teachers. So why was I so puzzled by this question? The cynic in me wondered if that word "autonomy" was a way of cueing me that there was only a slim connection between my administrative training and the requirements of this particular job. I further worried that there'd be little opportunity here for on-the-job training. So, was the real question, "Could I figure out this job on my own and assume responsibility for every mistake I made?" I did not share my characteristic painting of worst-case-scenario interpretations with my interviewer just yet. All of these musings occurred in nanoseconds.

"Could I be autonomous?" I quickly scanned my life for instances that would evidence some shred of autonomy as I understood it and I responded, "Yes." He smiled quietly, and I had that uncomfortable feeling when you realize you've responded too quickly to a question—that maybe you didn't fully understand the question—maybe you should have thought more about what it implied before answering. There was a discernible shift in the interview following my affirmative response. In that instant of responding "Yes," I began to imagine myself as the principal of Crow Island School. Slowly, I realized what was happening. I was becoming interested in this job—and he knew it.

LOOK INSIDE YOUR BACK POCKET

The interview continued to develop into an honest exchange of ideas and concerns. I openly shared my thoughts about the principalship as I had observed it in other schools. He talked about what the principalship should be—what the principalship could be—all the while studying my responses, both my nods and discomforts with his views.

He kept referring to my back pocket, that is, that all the matters I associated with being a principal (curriculum, budget, school law, community relations, organizational skills) should be available and easily referenced from my back pocket. But my leadership would be derived from something else—my ability to create and sustain a sense of community, my ability to advocate for children's needs, my ability to serve as both a resource to and a bridge between the teachers and parents.

He didn't talk in concrete terms about the principalship. There were no specifics. Rather, he talked about possibilities, community, large purposes, vision, and ideals. I was interested in what he had to say but not ready for it. I felt a wave of anxiety coming over me. The too practical side of me was wondering, if I did get this job, where would I go to get this kind of training by August? I was 33 years old—too young and naïve to realize that genuine autonomy, the central requisite for being a successful principal, comes from within.

MORE QUESTIONS AND THEN "THE WAIT"

A series of interviews and various types of meetings followed, with school board members, teachers, and parents. In each gathering, the unstated, bottom-line exchange of "Can she do it?" (their concern) and "What do they expect of me?" (my concern) permeated the dialogue.

I had no experience as a principal, so the "What would you do if . . ." kind of questions were particularly worrisome to me. I remember one question having to do with early dismissal of first-graders due to a recent change made in these students' dismissal time. "What did I think of this change and its effect on the children and teachers?" Truthfully, I had no opinion because I did not yet have a context for understanding the question. I was uncomfortable with my essentially "I don't know" response. Other questions included lengthy, descriptive lead-in statements that provided me with ample context for the question. I took that trait as a hopeful sign. I felt, for the most part, assisted in the interviews by the interviewers. As I listened more, and restrained my impulse to come up with the "correct answer," I began to realize that underneath all of these different queries and scenarios dwelled the same basic concerns, not specifically stated but strongly implied: Can you listen before you act? Will you care what we think? Can we trust you?

The prospect of assuming the leadership role in this school now fascinated me. I realized that I had been hooked (for better or for worse) and that I had undergone an important shift in both my concept of the principalship and my self-concept as well. After some anxious weeks of waiting, the superintendent called and offered me the job. I was thrilled to accept the position as the 12th principal of Crow Island School. Thrilled and terrified.

FIRST DAY FOR A NEW PRINCIPAL

The first day of my principalship was on Monday, August 13, 1984. I entered the building and maneuvered around the mountains of furniture in the hallways. The distant din of custodians at work in the far wings of the school could be heard. I went to the principal's office—my office now—and unlocked the door with the skeleton key given to me. The room was empty except for a wall of built-in cabinets. A black rotary-dial telephone sat forlornly on the floor.

At that moment, it occurred to me that I had never worked in a location separate from my immediate supervisor. How would he know I was here? I promptly reached down for the phone and called the secretary to the superintendent to let her know I had arrived and was on duty. She welcomed me warmly and assured me she would let the superintendent know I was here, but I sensed that she was suppressing an amused laugh at the formality and naïveté of my phone call. I needn't have checked in. I was to be autonomous—remember?

LEARNING TO LEAD FROM WITHIN

What should I be doing? I had no idea. It seemed completely weird to me to be the principal of an empty building on this August morning. There were no children. There were no teachers. I hungered for some human connection. I opened a cabinet that revealed the last few years of the faculty's group photos—neatly sequenced, labeled, and taped onto the inside of the door. I quickly found the faces of the teachers who had participated in my interview. I retrieved the faculty directory from one of the shelves, moved the black rotary-dial phone from the floor onto the wide windowsill (the only surface—there was no desk), and began dialing. From "Anderson, Donald" to "Warton, Dorothy," I called all of the faculty members I had not yet met. I introduced myself, asked how their summer was going, and said I was looking forward to meeting them soon. Many engaged me in further conversation. I was grateful to have this purposeful activity to consume these first hours on duty. As I dialed each staff member, I studied their faces in the successive years of group photos taped on that cabinet door, trying to get a sense of who these people were. How had they changed over the years represented in these photos? How did they relate to each other? What will our relationship be? I was struck by the age of the group as depicted in these photos. It seemed to be a mature group of teachers, overwhelmingly women, and I saw kindness in their expressions. My impression of the age of the faculty was later confirmed when someone told me I was the youngest person in the building. That fact did not bolster my confidence.

As I visited with each teacher on the phone, I heard their concerns. Some shared their perceptions of issues in the building. Others voiced a particular anxiety about the upcoming school year. I was so new to them that they had not yet assumed the caution in their communication with their administrator that would naturally come later. I wasn't even yet a face to most of them—just a voice, seeming to be friendly, wanting to help. I began to imagine their expectations of me in my role as their new principal.

In those first moments, days, and months of the job I imagined what kind of principal I would be. I promised myself I would be able to know, understand, and accommodate the needs of all the teachers, parents, and children. I would confront issues fairly, and although some would disagree with my decisions, they would understand and respect the process I used to make them. I would cultivate and develop teachers' ideas about curriculum and develop my own ideas as well. I would solve problems. I would listen. I would be a good principal.

INHERITING A SCHOOL

The beginning principal inherits a school—its students, staff, and community; the building; and what this school has become so far. You accept a school's strengths, joys, weaknesses, sensitivities, and needs. Brimming with fresh, nonpartisan energy, your initial work is defined by the expectations and urgent wishes of the long list of people you serve. You can't yet imagine that over the span of a career as principal everything you are as a human being will be fully called upon to prudently encompass the life of that build-ing, to shape it, and to influence its future. You will study that school, discover its secrets and ways of being. You will challenge its natural rhythms in the cause of moving toward a deeper recognition of what that school can be. And, hopefully, you'll recognize—and accept—what you're not able to change.

What you create—and more important, what all those for whom you are responsible create with you as their leader—will be a function of your ability to tolerate discomfort, uncertainty, and criticism until you find your center and the school's center as well. In those first hours, months, and even years of the principalship the notion of autonomy, the ability to be inner-directed, can only be in its infancy.

One of many ironies faced by the first-time principal (as well as for most leadership roles) is that in the beginning, it's too soon to know what you need to know in order to do the job well. The wisdom of experience doesn't exist separate and apart from the years of gleaning it. The process of becom-ing, of discovering who you are and how you'll lead, is a gradual unfolding that occurs in relationship with others—with teachers, with parents, and with children. Each decision, large and small, creates the path of your leader-ship, a path that becomes known to and relied upon by everyone you lead. Autonomy—the ability to be inner-directed in those decisions—may be the most powerful skill for principals to gain toward centering that leadership.

ABOUT MY SCHOOL

"*The Boss of the Whole School*": *Effective Leadership in Action* uses real school-life stories, gathered over my 21-year career, as the basis for examin-ing challenges to leadership that every principal, novice and veteran, faces. The setting of these particular stories is a small suburban elementary school of fewer than 500 students in an affluent suburb of Chicago. Class sizes of approximately 20 students are assigned to teachers, most with a graduate degree, who often spend an entire career in our school district. The Winnetka schools, currently comprised of 3 elementary schools and a middle school campus of two schools, servicing grades 5 and 6 and grades 7 and 8, respec-tively, have a long tradition of leadership in progressive public education (Washburne, 1952). The teachers are guided by that philosophical under-standing in the writing of curriculum and in their daily teaching. Through-out its history, the district's commitment to the consideration of the individual needs of the whole child and to the mastery of academic skills has been grounded in a firm belief in every child's ability to learn (*Crow Island School: Annual School Improvement Plan, 2004–2005*). Our community is proud of its schools. The parents are involved in the school's operation at many levels of a vast volunteer network. They are supportive and encouraging of a high standard of excellence in their children's education.

I fully realize the uniqueness of my school's circumstances and of my principalship. However, I began my career as a teacher in the Chicago Public Schools and so I've taken great time and care to choose lessons of leadership for this book that can be applied to school settings that present a great variety of challenges different in kind or degree from those I face. The reader will, hopefully, discover that the specific content of the stories, memos, or letters I've included can easily be used, with adjustments, in a wide variety of school settings. The usefulness of this material, however, is not necessarily connected to a particular school's physical location or enrollment or size of budget or kind of community. It's about a principal's visceral and psychical identification with being a person of responsibility. As a 21-year veteran, I know that a principal is a principal, no matter the particulars of our settings or circumstances. All schools everywhere require responsible leadership that promotes safety, a positive sense of community, and effective learning. The job of all principals is to help create a setting that acknowledges and supports the needs of the children, teachers, families, and community we serve. All principals assume the enormous responsibility for making that happen. Our contexts or paths or tools may look different, but our endpoints are identical.

THE LEADERSHIP JOURNEY OF THIS BOOK

This book is organized around what principals actually do each day to sustain and enrich the life of a school. The stories told have direct connections to dimensions of leadership, linking everyday occurrences to their larger potential for fostering the principal's own qualities as a leader and thereby the school's culture as a reflection of responsible professionalism.

This first chapter has set out the reader's itinerary for the chapters that follow by exploring the imagined hopes that a first-time school principal may experience. Chapters 2 and 3 are focused on the scaffolding work of the principal. Learning how to differentiate the priority of the leadership function from the demands of management is a necessary process that strengthens the school as a developing organism. Further foundational work for the principal is to create the rituals and traditions that sustain the life of a school and that signal values that bond individuals to larger purposes and a school's mission.

The middle of the book, chapters 4 and 5, are focused on the principal's work with teachers. Sharing leadership is a vital dimension of the collaborative relationship required between principal and teachers. Chapter 4 focuses on the faculty meeting, a key forum in which a school's leadership/followership plays out. I outline a process we used to transform much dreaded faculty meetings into revitalized and purposeful forums for defining and discussing issues of mutual concern. Strategies to navigate the day-to-day transactions with faculty and staff which encourage teachers to imagine along with you so that ideas can be shared and cultivated are included in this chapter. It begins with material previously published in *Phi Delta Kappan*. Chapter 5 is a lengthy examination of the teacher hiring process, perhaps the single most important task of a principal. Whether your district's hiring is conducted centrally or at each school, I include some basic how-to's about finding and hiring new teachers, and suggest a process to support their success.

Chapter 6 focuses on the relationship between students and principal and examines issues of student discipline. It also explains how a principal's leadership is required to shape the sense of moral community in your school. Chapter 7 is a lengthy and quite detailed look at one of the most visible and anxiety-producing roles of the principal, the placement of students into classes for the next school year. Anticipating the subtle intermix of children's needs, teachers' dispositions, and parents' expectations, and consolidating that thinking in the form of a classroom placement decision, will have a significant impact on each child's comfort, sense of security, and success in learning for each school year as well as the parents' regard for and trust in their principal's judgment.

Chapter 8, the initial inspiration for writing this book, takes a deep and personal look at administrative aloneness, its sources and realities, and offers some advice about how to cope with this not-so-wonderful aspect of the principal's job. Finally, in Chapter 9, I pass the baton on to my colleagues. Leaving a school is not an easy task. With luck, you are able to have enough warning to carefully and thoughtfully ready everyone—including yourself—for the transition. This predestined occurrence calls for the highest qualities of leadership, not just for one's self, but for the continuing benefit of the school. With a new principal in place a school reflects on its journey and continues its life, again shaped by new leadership.

At the close of each chapter, the reader will find a listing of its major concepts in a section entitled "Leadership Lessons." In between each chapter, I have included a "Clarifying Episode," a brief story intended to provide a glimpse of daily principal life that acclimates the reader to the leadership issues discussed in the subsequent chapter.

The principalship is a job of rhythms and cycles. The familiar rhythms of a school day and a school year are easily recognized by principals, new and veteran alike. But the ever-deepening cycle of apprehending leadership, taking ownership of leadership, and instilling leadership in others follows a less predictable calendar within the larger orbit of a career. Reflection on the evolution of our leadership is a required but often lonely process. It is helpful to know how others in that same role think about such matters. It is my hope that my reflections on the principal's leadership life in this book can be a companion to all who are or aspire to be a principal and who wish to examine and deepen their understanding of their leadership journey.

Clarifying Episode:
Painting the Pole

My first executive act as a principal is almost too embarrassing to relate. It may have been my third or fourth day on the job and I was walking around the building fulfilling my responsibility to "inspect the facility." Pondering my leadership goals was too daunting and even scary for me to attempt. I craved a safer management task to occupy my time.

School buildings are not pretty places in early August. The hallways still hold the evidence of the prior June's dirt and scuff marks. Piles of classroom furniture, custodial buckets with mop wringers, and wheeled carts to transport packages from one part of the school to another line the hallways. My eye was drawn to a support pole in the front foyer. Paint was peeling off of it, exposing dark metal blotches from floor to ceiling. Possibly jealous of those who were blessed with clearly defined tasks and responsibilities, I summoned the custodial crew to examine this disreputable pole, a glaring demerit for facilities management.

The head custodian, an older gentleman, glanced at the pole and then took a longer look at me. He realized that he had been called away from his duties not because of the pole, but rather because of what this new principal thought about this pole. He studied me for a moment. Clearly, he had worked for other principals and recognized my behavior as temporary and not too bothersome. So he humored me. That very afternoon, he set about the task of painting the pole. He arranged for me to select a color from a panoply of shades of white. Giving more time and far more attention than this project required or deserved, he threw out a large paint tarp on the floor of the foyer. He painted and repainted that pole, all the while looking to me for approval.

I carefully supervised that job and I remember feeling good about the outcome—a first success. I had identified a flaw and had acted decisively to correct it. Nobody noticed that the paint-peeled pole had been restored to its glistening white state. Nobody cared, or even noted, that it had become an eyesore for at least one person. That mattered little to me. For months afterward, I would walk by that pole, smiling and acknowledging that it was now beautiful—a hopeful harbinger of quick solutions to come.

2

Leading a School and Managing a School: What's the Difference?

Principals are always busy—really busy—but are we busy leading or managing? We are expected to be, first, the leader, but also the manager of our school. How are we to know what's leadership and what's management, and why do we need to know the difference? We attend endless workshops and seminars to better understand the tenets of leadership, during which time we are, ironically, constantly on our laptops and cell phones back to our schools—managing. Principals' energies are completely absorbed by urgent daily demands, while we are simultaneously haunted by a steady undercurrent of anxiety that we're always managing and rarely leading. Every principal is confounded by this riddle, the solution of which will have important consequences for our effectiveness. Take a deep breath, now, and see if you can solve this puzzle.

I WENT to my first yoga class today. I was amazed by this young instructor's extensive knowledge of how the body works. I was thinking I was there to stretch and relax. She had deeper purposes in mind. She assembled us into her gaze and demonstrated correct yoga breathing. Stomach—rib cage—chest. Chest—rib cage—stomach.

Halfway through the hour we gathered around her for a lesson about the foot. Did you know there are four pressure points on the foot—two on the balls of the foot and two on the heel? The teacher demonstrated the desired stand as centered between these four pressure points. The proper stand strives for alignment. She went on to show us misalignment, which is what most of us do, that is, we throw our weight on the sides of our feet. She pointed to her own foot and noted for us the surge of sanguine color on the side of her heel when she was in misalignment and the normal flesh tone of her heel when she was standing properly. I was captivated by this good teacher's clear instruction. My mind raced with application possibilities for this brilliant but simple fact of our physicality. It was still early in the summer, and clearly, I had not yet learned how to free my mind for yoga meditation.

FINDING MY LEADERSHIP FOOTING— CENTERED LEADERSHIP

It occurred to me that her lesson about correct standing translates directly to my work as a school principal. I am now many years into my life as a principal. Experience and maturity have awakened a deeper and complex perspective on my leadership role—a perspective I am now able to compare, with some humility, to my beginning naïve understanding of a principal's job.

Specifically, I was thinking about my dual roles of manager and leader of the school. I can quickly and easily describe my managerial role in excessive detail; but what about my leadership role? That aspect of my job is often fuzzy. I still find it difficult to wrap my mind around the concept of leadership, so I need images to support my thinking. This particularly clear yoga demonstration of proper standing suggested to me a mental framework for clarifying leadership, so I let my mind wander freely to connect the dots:

My leadership needs to be centered.

My centered leadership is an
extension of my values.

When my leadership is off-center,
exaggerated and often misdirected
surges of activity are the result.

When my leadership is balanced,
my energies are properly allocated,
distributed as needed
to span the crisis and the calm of the moment.

Centered leadership
is the goal
of the inner-directed school principal,
a goal rarely completely attained.

I am temporarily soothed by this deeper insight, fully knowing that my job seldom even approximates the level of peaceful reflection so present in the practice of yoga. The tensions, sudden emergencies, and multiple roles required of a school principal entail quite the reverse of the meditative state.

MANAGEMENT AND LEADERSHIP: WHAT'S THE DIFFERENCE?

I openly confess that I have been baffled for many years by the conundrum of the principal's leadership and management roles. Not unlike many if not most of my colleagues, I've struggled with balancing the pressing in-your-face demands of management with the siren-beckoning and transcendent claims of leadership. Even at a mid-career stage, most principals are still unable to merge these two roles successfully, but can nevertheless easily re-cite the attributes of each function:

Management focuses on solving problems with an efficient regard to time and resources, is quick-paced and immediate, and often requires a rapid-fire staging of responses.
Leadership both demands time and spans time. Its pace and rhythm are slow and reflective. Leadership seeks to examine problems and issues in depth, to identify possible connections with larger goals and initiatives of the organization, and to resolve problems within that larger context.

Then we confront that issue of time allocation. Truthfully, we don't need to allocate time for management. Principals know all too well that manage-ment will claim more than its fair share of time without any planning. So how to give leadership its due? When and how do we allocate time for that slower-paced rhythm that leadership requires? In just this way I continue to grapple with this circular puzzle.

At a time when this looming riddle was on my mind I happened to stop by a kindergarten classroom. I was greeted warmly and chanced upon one of our school's many rituals to promote a positive community: a rugtime con-versation about people's jobs in the school. Feeling that the timing of my visit couldn't be more perfect, the teacher smiled widely, grateful for this teachable moment, and asked her students: "Boys and girls, look who's here—our prin-cipal. What does the principal do?" At that particular moment I was seeking some clarification on that issue for myself and so I listened carefully. "She's the boss of the whole school," one girl stated with confidence. The others nodded in agreement, not needing to add anything else to that succinct de-scription of a principal's job. I gulped—"boss of the whole school" indeed.

BEING THE BOSS OF THE WHOLE SCHOOL

A child's understanding of what it means to be a boss barely touches the edges of the realities of a principal's job. A principal's day is characterized by interacting with hundreds of constituents and coping with events of all magnitudes that necessitate immediate decisions, crisis management, and constant watchfulness. The principalship is about simultaneous demands. For the most part, no individual task or duty is beyond my abilities. It's that constant yanking, however, from screen to screen; large to small; intimate to generic; crisis to detail; educational philosophy to mechanical systems of the building; 5-year-old to 45-year-old; classroom at the north end of the building to the farthest edge of the playground; coping with a parent's heated verbal assault to beaming with pride at a first-grader's first writing draft—it's that everything-at-the-same-time syndrome that wears me down and erodes my energy.

In the whirlwind of a normal school day, principals make constant decisions. We choose. We prioritize. We juggle. We manage. A simple decision about walking the hallways of our schools is influenced by how many tasks we can complete by choosing one hallway first rather than another. Principals are masterful at keeping both school schedules and staff schedules in mind as we negotiate our day. One 5-minute-walk down the west hallway in my school at 7:30 A.M. will allow me to check on the attendance in the Before-School Program, to acknowledge the staff members who faithfully supervise this program, to follow up on a conversation with a fourth-grade teacher who arrives early each morning, and to check on the leaky skylights in that wing of the building.

A school's boss is expected to be immersed in each microenvironment to solve problems, find solutions, encourage, support, and recognize problematic scenarios in their manageable size. You often accomplish these superheroic feats by simply walking around, listening, and noticing (Sergiovanni, 1996).

DAILY WALKS AROUND THE BUILDING:
GATHERING, SOLVING, AND ANTICIPATING PROBLEMS

There's a certain sacredness to these daily walks around the school. Like a bird-watcher collecting sightings of both common and noteworthy specimens and behaviors, the principal reaches into classrooms and hallways and gathers images, problems, joys, and disappointments. A principal ponders the meaning of these daily collections. The first sorting is by urgency and importance (which are usually not the same!). Principals often lament that the seemingly urgent becomes the important, thus relegating matters of true significance to a lower priority. Each day this environment changes if only in subtle ways. In these walks, in addition to relationship-building and problem-solving, a principal notes the ever-changing emotional ecology of the school.

I visit a classroom. The teacher is readying the children for a transition from a rugtime conversation to an activity time. I hear the concluding comments of what I'm sure was a lengthier discussion: "Do you think you can remember to use your helping words next time? Boys and girls, it's important that you follow the rules so that all of our friends can have a good time out on the playground. Okay now, it's activity time." As the children flow into their preassigned activities, I note the exasperated sigh of this veteran teacher. This particular group of boys and girls is taking longer to come together than others have. The teacher and I take a moment to scan the faces, and together we hypothesize some of the contributing factors. We fully realize the limitations of first impressions and so we make plans to have the social worker observe the group, give us some more wisdom, and then talk some more. What's been accomplished? We've acknowledged an issue—the most important step—and given each other permission to talk about it—an essential component of problem-solving.

It's unlikely that a teacher will have time to stop by your office to have this kind of conversation early enough so that the issues can be resolved. The fleeting transition from awareness of a dynamic to acknowledgment of a concern can easily be lost in the enormous number of and constant need for teacher–child interactions in the classroom and the normal and expected chaos that defines an early childhood classroom especially. In addition, if acknowledged, it exposes a teacher's vulnerability, further heightened by the deliberate act of going to see the principal. It is far easier for a teacher to have these kinds of incidental conversations in her own classroom, at a time when the comments have a meaningful context. Hearing the exasperated sigh of a veteran teacher is the cue that signals the principal to take advantage of the serendipitous timing of the visit and to support a teacher in positive ways.

On my way down the hallway, I spot our nurse with an armful of attendance sheets she is checking on personally. She stops me to say that Jessie is out again today, with no call from the parent. Our nurse is diligent about attendance calls and wishes the parents were as well. I promise to contact Jessie's mom and remind her of the procedure. At first, this problem seems minor to me; then I remind myself that a school nurse watches the school through a life-and-death lens. For a nurse, each departure from established procedure signals serious problems ahead. I am so grateful to have staff who maintain a strict focus on daily issues that easily fall off a principal's radar screen. There's so much to be done.

Heading back to my office, I eye a parent waiting outside her child's classroom for lunch dismissal. She is engaged in a heated conversation with another parent. My principal's bionic sense of hearing is activated, and I note upset in her voice as she relates some misunderstanding between her child and his teacher about an upcoming field trip. I know this parent, and I recognize that she is getting worked up and ready to unleash this upset onto the teacher who will soon open that door to dismiss her students. I resolve to have that not happen. There are few things as upsetting to a teacher's day as having a parent publicly berate you for some issue you are unaware of.

I stop to talk to this mom, acknowledge her upset, and support her as best I can simply by listening to her. The classroom door opens and the boy and his mom go home for lunch. He returns in the afternoon and happily boards the field trip bus with his classmates. Part of a principal's expected responsibility is to absorb upset feelings so that teachers can go about the more important work of teaching.

As I go about my days ruddered by the multiple expectations of the many constituencies I serve, I experience that momentary but quintessential anxiety that all principals have and then quickly set aside: "I'm busy . . . I'm really busy . . . but am I leading or only managing?"

A VIEW FROM THE BALCONY

As a school principal, I am not alone in my search for balanced leadership. There is an extensive literature on the topic of leadership that supports and advises leaders of organizations of all types and sizes. Donald Schön (1984), a social scientist and consultant, examines the problem-solving process that leaders utilize in five different professions—engineering, architecture, management, psychotherapy, and town planning. His well-known work defines the process of "reflection-in-action," the unstated problem-solving process that professionals actually use in their work. In another useful book, Ronald Heifetz and Marty Linsky (2002), Harvard University Business School leadership experts, describe a leader's critical need to gain perspective in the midst of action. These authors propose the useful metaphor of "getting off the dance floor and going to the balcony" to describe how a leader steps back to gain perspective while also remaining deeply engaged. Their metaphor refers to the leader's ability to assume a more meditative state while engaged in daily work.

> Achieving a balcony perspective means taking yourself out of the dance, in your mind, even if only for a moment. The only way you can gain both a clearer view of reality and some perspective on the bigger picture is by distancing yourself from the fray. (p. 53)

This is a particularly apt metaphor for school principals to consider. It guides us toward an inner-directed, autonomous style of leadership, one that interfaces management with leadership. Rather than isolating leadership from management as a strategy to insure their differentiated attention, Heifetz and Linsky's metaphor directs the leader to see the connections between the two. Moving to the balcony to gain perspective is a skill that, when practiced, allows a principal that brief moment to make that connection between management and leadership concerns. Being able to mentally vocalize the subtitles of what you are doing—"Okay, this is definitely leadership" or "I'm stuck in management again"—while you're doing it heightens your awareness and centers your energy.

FINDING TIME TO GET TO THE BALCONY

The amount of time a principal can devote to management of traffic, lunchroom, bus, and playground issues boggles the mind. If we think of these duties as connected to our leadership, however, we may discover that these responsibilities are endowed with some good "getting to the balcony time" when we can hone that leadership habit, pulling ourselves out of the action to get a better perspective on the life of our school.

Another opportunity to get to the balcony can be created by having a real person to talk to other than yourself. Inviting a critical colleague or a graduate student in leadership studies to shadow you throughout the day provides good balcony time. The presence of an interested colleague focusing on you and your work naturally heightens self-awareness. In the presence of an observer, you become especially attuned to the "what" and "why" of your management and leadership activities throughout the day. As you walk your building with a colleague, you find yourself commenting on your activities. This focused description of your work serves to assist the observer in understanding your purposes and style of leadership. More important, however, is that you hear yourself explaining what you're doing and why. This metacognitive narration has an amazingly salutary effect on your ability to maintain equilibrium and focus.

Of course, your routine solitary walks of the building (while you're engaged in problem-anticipating, problem-gathering, and problem-solving) provide excellent opportunities for moving to the balcony, *if you remember to go there*. Walk out of your office each day and breathe the life of your school. Start your day "on the balcony" and observe the school's nuanced changes since yesterday, last week, or last year. Witness the interactions of teacher to child, child to child, and teacher to teacher. Witness your own interactions as well. Talk with parents. Chat with the custodian. Be involved. Notice. Principals learn quickly that keeping an open door is insufficient to determine what's really going on in the school. You have to get caught up in its whirlwind activities in order to catch or sometimes elicit the casual musings, truncated ideas, and misunderstandings (and let's not forget the rumors!) that are traversing the school. All of these glimpses of a school's daily life are gathered up to be pondered and prioritized—their effects to be measured and managed by the principal.

As you're out and about the building—in that whirlwind—find even small opportunities to let people know how you think and what you value. It's helpful for staff and parents to get a peek at the human side of leadership.

VULNERABILITY—A GLIMPSE OF LEADERSHIP

Revealing your values is a particularly important aspect of the leader's responsibility. Not unlike most beginning leaders, I assumed that my expertise should be immediately visible and ever-present and that my vulnerabilities should be tucked away, well hidden from view. As a beginning principal, I measured the quality of my ideas, hopes, and dreams against a standard not yet revealed to me. I weighed the possible embarrassment of presenting an idea that wasn't good enough to the teachers; that "maybe they've already thought about that" anxiety seized my imagination and crippled my creativity.

I remember a particular faculty meeting in those early years. We were talking about children's writing, and the risk that children take in committing thoughts to paper. I wanted to bring the discussion to an adult level of comparison and so, with a great deal of hesitation, I shared some rejection letters I had received from a number of publishers for an article that I had submitted to their journals. Much like any group of children who are instantly fixed on their teacher when she begins a lesson with "I want to tell you a story about me," these teachers were fixed on me, wanting to know about this rejection. What did it mean to me? How did I handle it? Who am I? And, of course, the implicit "will you understand that we, too, can feel rejected?" As a beginning principal I had never felt closer to this group than I did at that moment, nor, I suspect, than they did to me.

On that day, at that meeting, I learned that the teachers needed to see my vulnerabilities. Vulnerability makes you human—the teachers need to see that side of you. Both expertise and vulnerability link you to the experienced lives and needs of the teachers you lead. Your expertise will develop and be demonstrated over time. Along the way, don't be shy about exposing some vulnerabilities that spur you onward toward the building of that expertise.

That glimpse of my vulnerability was firmly situated on the values of humane leadership—the zone of inner-directed autonomy from where all leadership emanates. I was, in that episode, leading in the sense of providing an image of my life as co-terminus to theirs, freeing all of us to be able to be truthful with each other, sympathetic to each other, able to open ourselves to each other, qualities essential to a trustful school atmosphere. Sure, that can be viewed as "managing" a needed dynamic. But it went far beyond that, to a level of shared insight that pervaded many of our ensuing interactions, me with them, each of them to each other. A level of value magnitude had been created that moved all of us in a desirable direction. The word "leadership" seems justified.

Of course, the school's leader needs to be judicious about sharing episodes of vulnerability. Letting the teachers know that you, too, find a particular parent challenging, or that occasionally you didn't handle a parent conference with as much diplomacy as you wished you had, lets the staff know that you recognize and relate to their challenges and dilemmas. Choose examples that fit that purpose and not examples that portray you as insensitive to confidentiality issues, as possibly incompetent, or as not in control of the building.

SOLVING THE LEADERSHIP–MANAGEMENT RIDDLE

Each day at 3:15 dismissal, I don my whistle and exit the front door. As I hurriedly walk down the hallway, I imagine thousands of principals performing this identical ritual—supervising traffic at dismissal. Our school has a small circular driveway that parents navigate to pick up their children. The configuration of this driveway has necessitated extensive planning and development of rules and procedures so that traffic flows freely and children are safely transported from the front steps of the school to their family's car, SUV, or some large-sized vehicle that is not yet labeled as a bus. (Veteran principals reading this description are shaking their heads in sympathetic understanding.)

Am I leading or am I managing? I consider under which heading to place "directing circle traffic." Each task, each project, each initiative fits the description for one of these categories. Isn't that right? The necessary but detailed, procedural tasks are management. The creative, generative, and foundational tasks and projects are leadership. I used to include directing traffic in the circle on my management list, a requirement of my duties as chief safety official of the school. But over the years I've come to realize that this specific daily ritual of overseeing traffic in the circle is subtly but firmly connected to my leadership. The visibility of the principal, the predictability of my presence in that traffic circle, punctuating the end of the school day and gathering up the miscellaneous issues that find voice at the close of school, are all important aspects of leadership that are fulfilled in that traffic watch. I lament the fact that I didn't have this insight 20 years ago.

I'm finally solving the riddle. Well, almost, anyway. I now know there is no neat and tidy differentiation between my dual roles of leader and manager. In fact, most, if not all, of what I do each day requires differing mixtures of the two. That sounds so simple. What's new for me is a deeper insight into the complex interconnection between the two roles, that is, how my leadership role influences my management role and vice versa. As long as I focus essentially on my leadership role, my management tasks are elevated to a purposeful context. However, when I focus primarily on my management function, my leadership role becomes disconnected and drifts away aimlessly. In that way a leadership focus can have an enhancing effect upon my management, but a management focus can have a disabling effect on my leadership.

This resolution to the puzzle, however, does not come without a cost. My life as a principal will not change unless I incorporate what I've learned into each day—every day. I must recognize that scarcity of time is and always will be a significant factor, and therefore I must adjust my habits and focus on tasks and projects that incorporate that significant blend of both the leadership and management strands. I may have to sacrifice the good feeling I have when arranging for that field trip bus to appear in front of the school as a result of several phone calls to the bus company, time-consuming calls that someone else can make. I may have to forego the staff's cheering approbation when I surgically retrieve a crumpled sheet of paper from a barely perceptible, less-known cavity of our much-beloved photocopier. Some of these tasks may have to be neglected in favor of those requiring ongoing vigilance associated with accomplishing large purposes over time.

That being said, there will be times when getting a very specific management task accomplished quickly and expertly stamps me as a leader—one who rises to a challenge with alacrity, one who is in command when needed to be. A significant key to the riddle is that the two dimensions of principalship may not always be separate from or in opposition with each other while; nevertheless, each is recognized and honored for its essential function. Leadership is the more compelling reason for a principal's being. However, it neither negates nor underestimates the role of management as one necessary dimension of effective leadership.

Continuing to wrestle with the leadership–management riddle can have a profound effect upon a principal's effectiveness, a project that will further clarify values associated with the principal and the school's mission. These values become recognized and embedded in a school's traditions and rituals that serve as recurring announcements of what's important in our school.

LEADERSHIP LESSONS

- School principals are expected to be, first, the leader but also the manager of the school, and yet the difference between these two roles is often not clearly understood by principals.
- An extensive literature on the topic of leadership explores the issue of how to differentiate leadership from management. Heifetz and Linsky (2002) propose the useful metaphor of "getting off the dance floor and going to the balcony" to describe how a leader steps back to gain perspective (leadership) while remaining deeply engaged (management).
- In carrying out daily routine management duties, principals have some good "getting-to-the-balcony time" when you can pull yourself out of the action and sharpen that mental habit of reflection in order to get a better perspective on the life of your school.
- Inviting an insightful colleague or a graduate student in leadership studies to shadow you throughout the day provides good balcony time. Commenting on the activities of your day in the presence of an interested colleague who is focusing on you and your work can have a profoundly positive effect on your leadership.
- Your routine daily walks of the building when you are visiting classrooms, as well as gathering, solving, and hopefully, preventing problems, provide excellent opportunities for "moving to the balcony." Walk out of your office each day and breathe the life of your school. Start your day "on the balcony" and observe the school's nuanced changes since yesterday, last week, or last year.
- Teachers need to understand that principals, too, have vulnerabilities. Vulnerability makes you human—the teachers need to see that side of you (but not too much) that lets the staff know that you recognize and are sympathetic to their challenges and dilemmas.
- There is no neat and tidy differentiation between the principal's dual roles of manager and leader of the school; most if not all of what we do each day is a blend of management and leadership. Awareness of the influences of each role upon the other is the key to solving the riddle and goes a long way toward strengthening the principal's effectiveness as a school leader.

Clarifying Episode:
The Ghost of Crow Island

*"Now that Halloween is here—Ghost of Crow Island please appear!"
Four hundred costumed children, first through fourth graders, are seated
in the outdoor amphitheater gazing up at the roof of the school in anticipation of a yearly tradition. With feigned impatience and now even louder
voices they repeat their chant. "Now that Halloween is here—Ghost of
Crow Island please appear!" The edge of a white sheet becomes visible.
Cheers begin to erupt. An image appears. An adult-sized, sheeted form
dances forward and waves to us. Immediately the children look around to
see which adult is not in their midst and therefore must be the ghost. Is it
Santiago, our much beloved head custodian? No, there he is. Which
teacher is not here? A few names are proposed. The assembled children
continue to clap and cheer. After a moment of playful waving and a few
dance steps, the ghost recedes from view and the children hurriedly make
their way to classrooms for their Halloween parties, confident they've
guessed the identity of this year's "Ghost of Crow Island."*

*Halloween is a big event at our school. Our school is adjacent to a
wooded area—a setting ripe for Halloween mystery. For many years the
school has had the tradition of an afternoon Halloween Walk through the
woods. This ghost character's premier appearance occurred my first year
and was the brainchild of our highly creative and imaginative music
teacher, who was also new to the school that year. In mid-October, in
preparing for the upcoming holiday, our imaginations found a meeting
ground in a few zany planning moments in my office. We created the
"voice" of a ghost to be carried over an old PA system as the children
began their Halloween parade. "Oooooooooooooo"—it was an instant
hit! The following year, teachers contributed further ideas. The actual
figure of a ghost took shape and has been with us ever since. A new
tradition was born.*

3

Creating Traditions:
How a School Gains an Identity

What do you remember about your elementary school's traditions? Did your school have a special Halloween assembly or other ceremonies to celebrate important holidays or transitions? Can you remember the words to your school's song? A school year is filled with countless classroom rituals, events, initiatives, and projects. Some are one-time events—others become traditions. How does that happen? A principal plays an essential role in modeling the values required to differentiate between the two. Recognizing the potential for individual events to become traditions that support a positive school culture is an important dimension of a principal's leadership role

STANDING AT THE FRONT DOOR

EACH MORNING I stand at the front door, greeting the children as they enter the building. "Good morning, Jake," "good morning, Katie—have a good one." The day begins. Most of the boys and girls acknowledge my greeting with at least eye contact, a still-sleepy smile, or a more animated "good morning" as they hurriedly make their way to their classroom hallways or to the playground for those last few precious moments of play before the whistle blows.

I watch children's faces. I observe their energy. I notice who walks into school with friends—who enters alone. I overhear the exchanges between siblings just before they separate to walk down grade-level hallways—another reminder of their differentiated school rituals. "Bye Lola . . . I love you," says Angelena as she waves to her first-grade sister.

A PRINCIPAL'S HABITS

Standing at the front door is one of those many habits that principals develop to incorporate routine into our own school day. Well-established rituals help to create at least a perception of longed-for boundaries for principals who know that the day will soon bring unanticipated problems and possible emergencies. Habits serve to stabilize us. That's the practical rationale for having them. Principals invent particular habits, routines, or personalized patterns of behavior in response to the normal chaotic events in a school that yank our attention and energies in multiple directions. We develop habits to exert some control over how those energies are directed.

More important, however, than serving as refuge for overburdened school leaders, these habits and rituals model values that principals wish to highlight in support of promoting a humane and thoughtful school atmosphere. In that way a principal's habits can serve as a model for rituals and traditions that assert control over a school's culture and stabilize the entire school's energies. For me, standing at the front door each morning serves that purpose. It's a habit that allows me to anticipate the school day— to preassess any impediments to what I judge to be the normal rhythm for this particular day's beginning. In addition, it models the value of the availability of the school leader. The predictability of my presence each morning is important for those looking for me. Teachers, parents, and students know they can find me at the front door at 8:30 each day if they need some help in getting their day started or to report anything they have noticed in these opening minutes. "Our teacher's not here yet." "Did somebody order a bus for our field trip?" "Any news about David's mom? Is she still in the hospital?" "Kevin needs to tell you about something that happened on the playground after school yesterday." "Can I leave a few minutes early for my dentist appointment in the city?" "I forgot my violin—can I call my mom?" "Some parents are in the office looking for you—they look upset."

These quick transactions at the front door—principal to child, principal to parent, principal to teacher, principal to staff member—are necessary as a way to help smooth out the rockiness of the day's start. Our receptionist's desk is nearby, and many of these issues can be researched and resolved with her assistance so that I can continue to maintain my watch at the front door. But mostly I'm there to watch the faces of the children— to anticipate their day on their behalf—to emphasize that central value as fundamental to a principal's role in the school. I observe an interaction, an expression; an unfamiliar dynamic, and I ask myself, "What am I seeing?" "What needs to be done? . . . or just remembered?" "Who needs to know what I just noticed?"

TELLING ON CHILDREN: WHO NEEDS TO KNOW?

Raymond enters school with a troubled frown, something I've noticed frequently over the past week or so. What just happened as he barreled out of that van? Raymond is reticent to provide any verbal explanation. But since I have witnessed this habitual start to Raymond's day so frequently, it requires my attention. Who needs to know?

I see a newly formed gathering of third-grade girls huddled each morning in the foyer, signaling a new social grouping. This gathering is now 3 days old, but they behave as if they've been meeting for years. Giddy with laughter and the tension that betrays each girl's uncertainty of the group's future, they are in spirited conversation. I watch to see if the animated but quieted voices are directed at any particular child. The nuanced, rapid-fire transitions of eight-year-old girls can easily surpass my imaginative reach. But even I know that something's up. Should I be concerned? Who needs to know?

Martha is climbing the front steps, and I note her habitual furrowed brow as she reaches the top step. Without a word, she follows closely behind another child who has pulled open the front door. With nothing in her own hands, I wonder why she doesn't open the door herself. "Good morning, Martha." She returns my greeting with a slightly anxious voice. She pauses again, this time waiting for a friend; no, actually, any first-grade classmate who walks down her hallway. It takes me several repetitions of this exact scenario before I realize that Martha never opens the front door herself and never walks the hallway to her classroom door without another classmate. She is consistently perplexed by both tasks. Is she unable to plan the motor movements to reach out, press down the door handle lever, and pull the door toward herself? Once inside, is she unable to remember which hallway leads to her classroom? As a former special education teacher, I watch her and wonder if Martha has a nonverbal learning disability. Who needs to know?

Patrick crosses the threshold sporting a fresh haircut. Before I can edit the effect of my comment, I blurt out, "Good morning Patrick—that's a handsome haircut." He continues to walk past me as he self-consciously runs the fingers of his right hand through the phantom curls of yesterday. His nervous side-to-side glance tells me he's thinking, "Who's going to tease me today?" Not a good way to start the day. Who should I tell? Who needs to know?

A SCHOOL'S WAY OF TELLING

Schools have highly refined communication networks that have operated successfully since long before the advent of e-mail. Teachers and principals appear in each other's doorways. We're accustomed to observing even a mild level of urgency in a principal's or teacher's demeanor that invites teachers to move toward the classroom door as they're giving directions to students in order to retrieve an important message, or directs a principal to abbreviate a phone conversation in order to respond to a teacher's expression that signals "something's up." As school people, these communication rituals are recognized as a reliable vehicle for busy teachers and principals.

And it's in just that way that I alert a 3rd-grade teacher to the new girls' social club in her classroom. "Oh yes," she responds knowingly, under her breath, to me and nodding her head. "We're working on that." Her response reminds me how thoroughly this veteran teacher knows her students and how unlikely it would be that I could provide her with a newsworthy bulletin. Still, good to check. And it's in just that way that our physical education teacher learns of Patrick's haircut during his first-period class. "Patrick's got a new haircut—he's worried about getting teased," I whisper. "Okay—good to know" is his response.

A quick conversation with Raymond's teacher puts my morning observation in a larger context. In fact, Raymond does talk to his teacher about his difficult mornings, and she is monitoring this situation. And a note to Martha's teacher and the psychologist sets in motion a very necessary series of conversations and meetings about what is later confirmed to be a significant learning disability.

Each day an enormous amount of information about children is exchanged. These conversations and messages serve first and foremost to help children. In addition, these communications serve to refine teachers' and a principal's observations of children so that our collective experiences become a rich reference for all faculty and staff in the school, and that collective professional ethos itself becomes a cherished school tradition.

School people operate in this way. We quickly sort out which messages are *now*, which are *before lunch*, which are *today*, which are *when we get around to it*. We assess which messages are face-to-face, which are e-mail, and which are to be placed in mailboxes. The efficiency of this network never ceases to amaze me, and I need to remember to never underestimate the highly refined spirit of community that is required in order for this communication circuitry to be activated. This information network serves the essential purpose of making school a safe environment for children— and for adults as well. The tradition of being known is so important for children. Having confidence that the adults in your school are watching you and looking out for you helps to ease the challenges children face each day.

THE IMPORTANCE OF KNOWING AND BEING KNOWN

In our sincere wish to provide a safe, pleasant, and nurturing environment for children, we have discovered that school traditions and classroom rituals can act as purposeful signal markers that identify a clear path toward the development of relationships and gaining confidence. A personalized and genuine emphasis on values of community and friendship has a direct linkage to our children's feelings of safety.

Over the years we have developed rituals and traditions that remind us that children (and adults, too!) require a welcoming environment to help ease the transition into their new school or even a new school year. Shortly after the school year begins, all of the staff and students come together in the auditorium for our annual "Welcome Assembly." The purpose of this gathering is to introduce all students and staff members who are new to our school. In preparation for this assembly, each child or adult who is new to the school is interviewed by a classmate or colleague. "Where are you from?" "What do you like to do when you're not in school?" "Do you have any pets?" "What's your favorite food?" are among the questions that elicit the much-anticipated assembly introductions.

We begin with teachers and staff so that children can feel secure in having the process modeled for them. Current faculty and staff members introduce new faculty and staff to the gathered school community. "Hi, boys and girls, I'm Ms. Brownell. I teach second grade and I would like to introduce you to Ms. Jessica Newport, a new second-grade teacher. Ms. Newport lives in Chicago and she taught kindergarten at the Roycemore School. And you'll want to know that Ms. Newport is a dancer. She appeared in a ballet and she still takes dancing lessons."

"Hi boys and girls, I'm Mrs. Wimer, and this is Miss Lambert, and she'll be an Assistant Teacher in my 1st grade classroom. Miss Lambert lives in Evanston, and she has a dog named Oliver. Her favorite food is spaghetti." "I'm Ms. Gmitro, your music teacher, and I would like to introduce Ms. Lillian Phipps, our new Art Teacher. Ms. Phipps lives in Chicago and she enjoys scuba diving. Her favorite food is pizza."

After all the new faculty and staff members have been introduced, the teachers return to their seats and, starting with the first-graders, the children and their introducers come to the front of the auditorium. These youngest children are accompanied by their teachers, and as the microphone is handed to each child they proudly begin their introduction. Assisted by whispers from their teacher and reminders from the new child, each introducing child feels the sense of support and success that we are hoping to communicate to everyone. "This is Catherine. She's from Michigan and she likes to play soccer." As each grade level completes their introductions, the teachers marvel at the evolution of maturity unfolding right before our eyes. First-graders grasp the microphone with teachers whispering in their ears. Second-graders don't require the physical presence of the teacher, but are glad to have them nearby mouthing reminders. Third-graders introduce new students capably, giggling over some mispronunciations or omissions. And finally, our fourth-graders, looking like young TV anchors, feel the confidence to introduce themselves and be somewhat playful with the audience: "Hi, I'm Harry, and I'd like to welcome Ted. He went to school in New York and, already, he likes our school better. Glad to have you with us, Ted."

MUSIC CONVEYS COMMUNITY

To punctuate the strong feeling of community, at the close of the assembly we sing our school song, "Good Old Crow Island":

> Good old Crow Island
> The best school ever made, yes
> Good old Crow Island
> From kindergarten to fourth grade.
> The building's not too low or tall
> It's just right you might say.
> And because it is the best of all
> We enjoy it every day.
> —Helen Long

Our school song, in fact written by a former student in the 1960s, serves to anchor our sense of community and reinforces our need to belong to something larger than ourselves.

Music plays an important role in our school's memorable traditions by adding a particular depth of emotion and bond of community. Regularly scheduled music assemblies and gatherings contribute ritual in a manner not accomplished by any other facet of our school life. Our annual Spring Sings are a much-anticipated event, when children's imaginations and ideas for a particular grade level's program theme are transformed into an innovative presentation of artistic scenes and sounds under the skillful and creative direction of our music teacher.

REFLECTIONS IN THE WEEKLY BULLETIN

Like most schools, we have a weekly newsletter, *The Crow Island Bulletin*, that goes home to parents to notify them about upcoming events and deadlines and to convey the usual seasonal reminders to "be sure your child has an extra change of clothes in the locker" and "check the lost and found for long-forgotten sweatshirts, mittens, and lunch bags." Many years ago, it occurred to us that this weekly communication could be useful in acquainting parents with our school, with our curriculum, and with us, as well. So we asked parents to enter the dialogue of reflection so that we become known to each other as we collaboratively plan the school lives of their children. With these goals in mind, we include an occasional piece written by a faculty or staff member or parent. Initially, these writings described, for example, reading programs and science lessons and their relevance to our curriculum. Gradually, over a period of years, these weekly submissions have become a vehicle for clarifying our own thinking about teaching and raising issues of importance to us—both teachers and parents. These reflections have become another tradition by which we come to know one another.

PARENT TO PARENT

A well-organized system of parent volunteers is invaluable to a school's success. We have an extraordinarily well-organized parent organization. Over the years, committees have been created that support projects and initiatives that contribute to a positive school culture. The *Bulletin* is published weekly by one of our parent committees. This tradition serves as the information lifeline to parents about school events and issues. By noon on Friday, all submissions are contained in the large green envelope in the parent organization's designated mailbox in the front office. The *Bulletin* committee formats the information submitted, including a calendar of events for the coming week, and delivers the final draft on Monday morning. Copies are run in our district's publications department and the *Bulletin* committee members return to school on Tuesday to place packets of the *Bulletin* into teacher mailboxes so that children take it home that day. To save on cost, one child in the family (the youngest) is the designated "backpack messenger" of the weekly *Bulletin*. Recently, this forward-looking committee has made the *Bulletin* available to parents via e-mail.

A recently formed parent mentoring committee has been successful in making our many new families feel welcome and supported. Modeled after our teachers' mentoring program, a parent committee matches new families with a current family having children of similar ages and living near the new family. The mentoring family has been given a list of tasks and responsibilities, including highlights of that grade level that are often not written down anywhere but come to be known as helpful hints for parents to pass on to others: "Remember to wear your Mother's Day necklace at school events." "Your third-grader will have lots to share with you after their day in the

Pioneer Room. Be sure to set aside time." "A rainy day in the traffic circle is an experience you may want to avoid." These are just a few of the tidbits of school lore that parents need to know and are faithfully communicated by our parent mentors.

YOU'RE BACK—HIP-HIP-HOORAY!

Children delight in getting to know the other boys and girls in their classroom. Each classroom has its own rituals to promote a sense of positive well-being and community. A welcome-back song is heard each morning in one kindergarten classroom to support any student reentering the classroom after an illness or absence. Many of our classrooms include a custom that highlights each student in some autobiographical ceremony. Whether it's "Star of the Week" or "Person of the Week," these are designated times in the classroom routine for children to gather their thoughts about their own hobbies, a favorite book, or selected possessions, and share these reflections with classmates assisted by their teacher. Classroom yearbooks are another way of attributing importance to knowing each other. The basic idea is for each child to interview a classmate and write a brief half-page summary of that conversation. The teacher then compiles these student biographies, including a photograph of each child, into a laminated and spiraled booklet. The teacher photocopies the booklet so that each child will receive a copy. The original yearbook becomes part of the classroom's library. Variations of this practice may include a group photo or a drawing instead of individual photographs and stapling sheets together instead of spiraling.

Second-graders study biographies. To support these students' understanding of personal narratives, their teachers arrange for each 2nd grader to interview various people in the school. During that winter week of biography study, 2nd graders are found throughout the building scheduling appointments and developing their interview skills as they learn more about the lives of the art teacher, custodian, principal, school secretary, crossing guard, and nurse, to name only a few of the school staff celebrated in these child publications. What's your first name? When were you born? What do you like most about your job? What's the most embarrassing thing that ever happened to you? are the questions posed by these child interviewers that depict their age-appropriate interests in our lives.

FACULTY AND STAFF WALL OF FAME

To further support our tradition of getting to know each other, one faculty member suggested that we create a Faculty and Staff Wall of Fame. Each staff member prepares a biographical sheet that includes information such as hobbies, first job, favorite book, and so on. The sheet also includes a picture with family or a photo as a child. After 2 years of talking about it, we finally managed to organize ourselves to prepare these sheets, beautifully displayed by our art teacher on banners in our main hallway. On the first morning that the banners appear every year, many teachers and staff members can be found in that hallway studying the names and enjoying the lives of their colleagues as shown in their photographs. The children eagerly search for the banners that include their teachers to learn more about their lives, children, hobbies, and interests. Figure 3.1 is a reproduction of the form the biographical sheets are based on.

STUDENT PORTFOLIOS: KNOWING YOURSELF

About twenty years ago, we decided to encourage our students to gather their work over time so that they could see evidence of their own learning. We were inspired by many articles and dialogues appearing in various journals about portfolios and so we began a project with student portfolios at Crow Island—one that has become a major tradition in our school not only to focus on children's learning but also to involve teachers and parents.

When we started this project we didn't fully understand the enormous possibilities that portfolios could offer. The notion that there could be some child-centered, qualitative supplement to the single-number characterizations of learning, as expressed in test scores and as emphasized by our testing culture, seemed reason enough to organize our efforts and our students' efforts. The idea of collecting more substantive evidence of our curriculum and teaching initiatives to counteract narrowly defined test scores seemed innovative in the mid-1980s. What we couldn't comprehend at that time is that the process of selecting samples of their own work into a portfolio is profoundly important to children. We learned that all children have a natural ability and desire to tell their story as expressed in the contents of their portfolio. Even now, we are still excited about capturing the individual voices of our students through portfolio collections. Portfolios have become a vehicle for our students to know themselves as learners. In addition, portfolios are now embedded in our identity as a school—they are a significant part of our school's story. (That story, and its implications for staff development, is told in another book. See Hebert, 2001).

PRINCIPAL'S LETTER TO STUDENTS

Coming to the close of the elementary years is an emotionally charged experience for our fourth-graders. Most of the children have been with us for

FIGURE 3.1. Wall of Fame Memo

To: All Staff

Every year, we put up a faculty/staff "Wall of Fame" that includes photos and facts about each of us. Please fill out the attached form, paste on a photo, and return to Lillian. The photo can be a recent photo or even one from childhood. It's up to you.

Thanks!

(YOUR PHOTO)

Name:

Job at Crow Island:

My first job:

My favorite book:

My favorite food:

My favorite thing(s) to do when I was in elementary school:

My favorite thing(s) to do now:

5 years and their last year is filled with special experiences, including their Portfolio Evening with parents, an evening set aside for each child to share their portfolio with their own parents. As one of their many loving cheerleaders, I take this opportunity to write a letter to each child that reviews the list of teachers they had as they have progressed through the grades as well as something I particularly remember or appreciate about them. (See figure 3.2 for an example of a letter.)

These letters serve as my acknowledgment of each student's journey through our school and my wish that children remember that they were noticed and known by their principal.

FIGURE 3.2. Principal's Portfolio Letter to Students

Dear Susan,

Congratulations on coming to the final weeks of your 4th-grade year at Crow Island School. You are a member of a great class of students, and I have very fond memories of all of you over the past years.

My earliest memory of you is when you were sitting on Mrs. Widlicka's Kindergarten rug. You learned a lot about reading in Ms. Tarini's 1st grade. In Mrs. Ng's 2nd grade you helped organize the classroom store in your study of economics. I'm sure you'll never forget spending a day in the Pioneer Room with Miss Schoeller. Now you're preparing for your last Portfolio Evening in Mrs. Drew's 4th-grade class.

I'm glad you participated on the *Crow's Caw* staff. Your Science Fair Project, "The Solar System," was well done and sparked a lot of interest. The 4th-grade songs in this year's Spring Sing, *The Crow Island Music Awards,* were so creative and enjoyed by everyone. And Mrs. Wimer's 1st-grade students will always remember your class as their 4th-grade buddies.

I will remember you especially, Susan, for your cheerful disposition that has remained unchanged since you entered Kindergarten. I still have a copy of that video tape your dad made when you were in Wisconsin and you learned how to prepare maple syrup. You have so many talents and abilities. You are a strong writer, an excellent musician, and a positive leader—what a combination! I will miss seeing you next year in the halls of Crow Island.

I am very proud of you and I appreciate all that you have shared with us at Crow Island over these past years. I wish you all the best in your middle school years and continued success in all that you do.

With love,

Dr. Hebert

WHILE IT'S FRESH

A useful strategy to help a principal support a school event becoming a school tradition is to elicit quick staff comments about that event or project via a "While It's Fresh" memo. Immediately following events in the school (e.g., Welcome Assembly, Poetry Gathering, Halloween Walk through the woods, The Run-A-Thon, Fourth- & First-Grade Buddy Events), I slip a "While It's Fresh" memo in all staff mailboxes. "While It's Fresh in your mind please give me feedback about (*event*)." "What worked well?" "What didn't work well?" "Suggestions for improving this event?" "Comments?" In addition to establishing traditions, the "While It's Fresh" feedback is also helpful in fine-tuning the more routine activities throughout the school year that can always use a second set of eyes (e.g., school pictures, state testing, an assembly, fire drills, the new voice mail system). Getting into the habit of getting feedback from your staff lets people know that their opinions, suggestions, and comments matter. Following up by implementing suggested changes (and reminding staff that you did just that) demonstrates to students, teachers, and staff that their thinking is valuable and that their principal makes things happen; that their principal leads.

GAINING AN IDENTITY THROUGH
TRADITIONS AND RITUALS

A school's culture, including its rituals and traditions, doesn't just happen—it evolves out of a carefully designed child-centered environment. Hugh Price (2005), educator and author, notes the critical importance of ritual in the life of a community: "Communities cling steadfastly to rituals and rites of passage because they are powerful vehicles for celebrating accomplishment and transmitting cherished values from one generation to the next" (p. 35). Countless numbers of books and articles about school leadership support the notion that principals provide leadership in creating a positive school culture. No principal would disagree with that ideal. Sustaining that positive school culture, however, is simply too large a task for any one person. Promoting that positive school culture is best accomplished when everyone shares the responsibility for doing so. Cultivating a shared leadership atmosphere in the school promotes the kind of positive culture in which principal, teachers, and parents are working to achieve common goals.

LEADERSHIP LESSONS

- Recognizing the potential for some individual school events to become possible traditions that convey fundamental values to support a positive school culture is an important dimension of a principal's leadership role.
- Principals invent particular habits, routines, or personalized patterns of behavior in response to the normal chaotic events in a school that divert our attention and energies in so many directions. We develop habits, like standing at the front door each morning, to exert some control over how those energies are directed. These habits stabilize us. Traditions and rituals serve the same function for the entire school.
- A principal's tradition of standing at the front door or being on duty in the hallways each morning is one of many that serves to announce to the entire school community that knowing the students is important.
- An enormous amount of information about children is exchanged between principal and teachers every day. These conversations and messages serve first and foremost to help children. But they also serve to refine adults' observations of children so that our collective experiences become a rich reference for all faculty and staff in the school. And that collective professional ethos itself becomes a cherished school tradition.
- School people quickly and efficiently sort out which messages are *now*, which are *before lunch*, which are *today*, and which are *when we get around to it*. We assess which messages are face-to-face, which are e-mail, and which messages are to be placed in mailboxes. This efficient information network ritual serves the essential purpose of making school a safe environment for children—and for adults as well.
- In our sincere wish to provide a safe, pleasant, and nurturing environment for children, we have discovered that school traditions and classroom rituals can act as purposeful signal markers that identify a clear path toward the development of relationships and gaining confidence. A personalized and genuine emphasis on values of community and friendship has a direct linkage to our children's feelings of safety.
- A school's rituals and traditions, such as the beginning-of-the-year all-school-welcome assembly, the school song, an all-school parent newsletter, a parent mentoring committee, a classroom welcome-back song, a classroom star of the week, classroom yearbooks, students' interviews of teachers and staff, a faculty and staff wall of fame, music programs and assemblies, student portfolios, the principal's letters to graduating students, and many others that schools have established, create a genuine community in which all have a stake and that all can cherish while in the school throughout life.

Clarifying Episode:
Teachers as Leaders

All the signs were there—those unmistakable signals that something was different. The teachers appeared in the faculty room promptly at 11:40. On time. That was different. There was a noticeable quiet and excitement. They didn't line up at the microwave to heat up a three-course lunch. Today, somehow they remembered to bring a sandwich or a piece of fruit that didn't require much preparation.

Today was important—not a moment to lose. Everyone quickly took a seat and focused their attention on their colleague standing before them—a new voice of leadership. Melissa, a first-grade teacher, also a member of the Safe-to-Learn Committee, was our facilitator for today's staff meeting. We had agreed to change the format of our faculty meetings—to select a single topic and have different teachers act as facilitators to lead our discussions and to probe them further. Melissa had volunteered to facilitate this week's faculty meeting on the topic of playground behavior and emotional safety.

Nervous, but gaining her confidence, this teacher leader began to speak. "Hi, everyone—okay, let's get started." The expression on her face was a clear indication to me that she was experiencing that first discernible discomfort and anxiety of leadership: "Will they listen?" "Will I remember what I wanted to say?" "Will I forget to acknowledge someone?" "Can I do this?"

She did remember what she wanted to say, and they all listened attentively. These teachers' interest and positive contributions to the meeting were energized by their own notion of leadership by proxy—a designated teacher as leader. Melissa assumed this responsibility with care and collegial obligation. She carried it out beautifully. The teachers applauded her premier leadership performance—the first of many to follow.

4

Rugtime for Teachers: Reinventing the Faculty Meeting and Mentoring Good Ideas

---

A principal's ideas invite close scrutiny from the teachers, especially ideas that suggest change! A few years ago I changed the format of our faculty meetings. I eliminated the long list of random announcements with which we felt compelled to start our twice-monthly meetings. I was confident that we had other (and better) vehicles to communicate the information in these announcements. I felt that beginning each meeting with an uncertain number and wide variety of announcements significantly abbreviated our time together, time best used to focus on discussion of mutually important topics. This chapter begins with an article I wrote about reinventing our faculty meeting (Hebert, 1999). The second half of the chapter revisits that story and recounts some lessons to be learned from it.

I confess! For almost two decades I have not looked forward to faculty meetings. Over all this time, I've allowed our meetings to go the way of the stereotypic faculty meeting—dreaded mandated gatherings that jolt us from our teaching day into a 50-minute rapid firing of disconnected announcements and abbreviated discussions about issues that require much more time and thought.

I've attempted a number of different formats over the years to break out of the rut, but all have yielded pretty much the same mediocre results. Whether it's the "preannounced agenda list" or the "faculty committee to propose the agenda" or the "open-ended let's see what's important to everyone approach," these meetings have failed to capture the hearts and minds of the faculty . . . or the principal, for that matter!

DREADED FACULTY MEETINGS

Why have these faculty meetings become so dreaded? Because I sacrificed our meeting times for ordinary purposes, which inevitably yield ordinary results. I lost sight of the importance of using what precious little time we have together for refining and reinforcing our understanding of and commitment to the kind of positive faculty community that is so required of a good school. I abandoned the complexity of my leadership role in guiding us toward this essential goal and, instead, I maintained the conventional role of agenda composer, timekeeper, and taskmaster. I led the meeting, responded to questions about how we would resolve issues, and clarified announcements as needed.

This format is not unpredictable in schools and may even be thought of as soothing and comforting for many teachers. The principal leads and the faculty follows—what could be easier or more expected? It's easier because active involvement is not required. It's expected because, after all, the principal is supposed to run the school, right?

It began to dawn on me that, contrary to my convictions about the kind of collaborative leader I hoped to be, I was unintentionally reinforcing a leader–follower dynamic that tends to produce a division between principal and faculty and a not-to-be encouraged dependence on the principal for resolving matters best addressed by the teachers, possibly with a principal's advice. I am keenly aware of the complexity of the relationship between faculty and principal and its consequences for the life of a school, and I was just now beginning to realize that our faculty meetings were demonstrating an opposite and unintended leadership style. Although subtle, the underlying tone was counterproductive to the natural sense of sharing that we enjoy when we're not involved in these meetings. It was becoming abundantly clear to me that the format of our meetings did not serve our collaborative purposes. It was time to consider a new format.

CHILDREN'S RUGTIME MEETINGS: A FULFILLING COLLABORATION

At a particular moment when I was mulling over this issue, I was visiting a 1st-grade classroom. The teacher was gathering her students for a rugtime meeting. As the first-graders purposefully assumed their positions around the perimeter of the rug I attended closely to the dynamics of this assemblage. What makes a good rugtime meeting so compelling and fulfilling for the children and teacher? Well, first, the children all know one another. They have a common history and they share common experiences. They have numerous opportunities to interact and collaborate. Each day these children are better able to predict each other's responses to the events of a school day, thereby learning more about the most important lesson they feel they can learn: how to make friends.

At this particular rugtime meeting, the topic of discussion was the design of the courtyard garden. The children were presented with the enviable task of redesigning the courtyard garden outside their classroom. Young children gravitate to the authenticity of such a project, and they are both grateful for the opportunity for real work and aware of their collective competence to fulfill this obligation. As I observed their ideas being carefully recorded by their teacher onto chart paper, I witnessed these children making a significant interpersonal transition. The usual random announcements made by students about weekend events, play-dates, and newly acquired toys were postponed because a new and important agenda had been presented. Those incidental communications could easily be shared at another time during the day. Now the children were actively engaged in careful listening to one another, making sure that each comment or suggestion was relevant to the plan for the courtyard. Listening carefully, focusing on a communal goal larger than one's own needs, contributing to a shared solution beneficial to all members of a caring community: all these are major developmental tasks for first-graders. I wondered if the teachers could accomplish an equally momentous developmental task at our meetings. Could we emulate the maturational challenges presented to these 1st graders? What we needed, I began to realize, was a focus on creating solutions to meaningful problems and issues we all shared.

SIZE OF THE GROUP MATTERS

Making friends—developing a community of people who care for one another—is a need unrelated to a person's age. It is, however, a need that is more easily fulfilled in groups of modest size. Over the past few years our faculty has grown in response to increasing student enrollment. Once a very small school, we have come to realize with embarrassment that we don't all know each other very well anymore. The acknowledgment of our relative largeness and its consequences has become a recurring theme in our faculty conversations as our awareness grows of the dangers of losing what Deborah Meier (1996) has so eloquently alluded to as "the benefits of smallness."

> Smallness is a prerequisite for the climate and culture that we need to develop . . . authentic relationships built on face-to-face conversations by people engaged in common work and common work standards. . . . A good school is

never satisfied with itself. As a result, there's never enough time. But it turns out that everything is easier when we get the scale right. (p. 12)

I began to suspect that we already had some of that wisdom in place, but we didn't recognize it. In our very first staff meeting of each year we engage in a ritual of coming together in our faculty room, chairs arranged in a circle, and luxuriating in an important task: Each staff member takes whatever time they'd like to introduce or reintroduce themselves to the group of continuing and new faculty and staff. What I now recognize as our first rugtime of the year is always anticipated as an intimate gathering of 70 or so colleagues who are most anxious to see one another once again for another year and to welcome new members to the group as well. The purpose is not exclusively social, although that is always a welcomed positive outcome.

Our increased size has also caused us to become more conscious about communication in general. We have become more deliberate about getting information into each other's mailboxes. [At the time of this article we did not yet have access to e-mail.] Announcements are often crucial, and we have developed vehicles for conveying them. In addition to my weekly memo, we have come to regard a single metal bookend on the office counter as a communication lifeline. Each day at least one message is clipped to it for all to receive as they fly through the office on their way to the photocopier or the staff lounge. "Indoor recess today!" "Melissa had a baby girl." "Where's the long-arm stapler?" "Len is out; no sub, sorry!" These are all the unanticipated important pieces of news that form the daily life of a school. So we have intuitively figured out how to handle the transmission of important messages and announcements.

LEAPING TO A NEW FORMAT FOR FACULTY MEETINGS— NO ANNOUNCEMENTS!

I felt that we were now ready to confront fundamental issues and make the leap into a new kind of faculty meeting—a rugtime meeting for teachers. Drawing on the rugtime spirit of our own initial meeting of the year and witnessing the possibilities after attending the first-graders' rugtime meeting in the fall, I wrote a memo to faculty listing the dates of our meetings for the year together with a request that we attempt a new format—single-topic reflections and discussion. With this proposed plan, topics would be suggested by faculty and principal. A single topic would be selected and announced in advance of each meeting so that we would have opportunity to gather our thoughts on that theme. With this new format we would eliminate all announcements at our meetings so as not to use up our precious time together for purposes best achieved by being faithful to our mailboxes and the bookend clip on the office counter, and we would ensure a focus on a concern shared by all of us.

I have learned over the years to rely upon the strong and thoughtful sense of professionalism of the teachers at Crow Island. They have a tactful style of detecting issues requiring attention and sharing observations with each other and with me as appropriate. My job is to catch these remarks, often given in the most casual manner, and recognize them as a signal for our collective readiness for change. I must be mindful that the distance between one teacher's casual remark and an entire faculty's readiness for change can be likened to a tightrope that must be traveled with intention and patience. As principal, my job is to discern the clear path from the perception of disequilibrium to the resolution of balance without complicating the process with other issues.

GATHERING TOPICS AND IDEAS TO DISCUSS

I listened for topics and ideas and didn't have to wait long. Prior topics resurfaced quickly with the hope of more time for discussion, and new subjects evolved out of hallway conversations. The teachers wanted to talk about the heightened sense of competition our first-graders experience on Field Day. They also wished to spend some time together talking about the recent death of a child's parent. What words should we use to support that child and his classmates in this tragic event? How do we respond to children's questions about death and loss? Other topics emerged quickly. Due to growing enrollment, it is clear that our fifth-graders will be moving over to the reopened middle school. This move won't happen for a year, so teachers want to talk about planning for this huge change. Which teachers will go to the middle school? How will that decision be made? How will we ready our fourth-graders for a move to the middle school? What elementary school traditions and rituals will they miss, and what special attention can we put in place for this particular group of fourth-graders? How will we decide?

As principal, my role in defining and nurturing productive issues for discussion and, in particular, a topic as comprehensive as a demographic shift in our school is, first, to pluck it out of the many chaotic conversations in hallways and name it as a topic of importance and mutual concern. Once designated as a topic, the principal's job is to calm people down, respond to all the misinformed rumors, and lay out a process for staff to use to uncover and discuss the many layers of concerns this topic involves. In this case our discussions revealed unsettled feelings experienced by some teachers, a wealth of creative and purposeful ideas to support our fourth-graders and their parents, and a ton of details to attend to in preparation for the move. It also clarified that breaking into a small group format was effective and should be considered for other meetings as well.

SHARING LEADERSHIP: HEARING ALL VOICES

Sharing leadership is a vital dimension of a principal's role. It acknowledges the collaborative relationship required between principal and teachers, all of whom share the goal of developing and sustaining a positive school culture. Moving beyond the expected "principal as leader and teachers as followers" dynamics to a shared leadership model introduces a new dynamic of interrelations where new voices of leadership can emerge. The reconceived faculty meetings were an ideal basis for encouraging teachers to assume leadership in regard to central issues of our school community.

What did we learn from our rugtime meetings? Clearly, we all observed positive changes. Narrowing the focus of our discussion has the effect of making the group seem smaller. We're gaining some facility in differentiating which topics are best handled by breaking into small groups rather than always conducting whole-group discussions.

There is now a palpable focus in the group that is attributable to our genuine interest in hearing one another—and ourselves—think about common issues. We are energized as we find support and encouragement from one another for our sometimes convergent and sometimes divergent views. In all of our discussions it is abundantly clear that who we are as people deeply affects our teaching as well as our ability to be a good colleague. We listen to one another to affirm our thoughts, to challenge our thoughts, to think new thoughts. The process is revitalizing, but it requires energy, courage, and, most important, feelings of safety.

Clearly, all teachers will not enter a group discussion with common feelings of safety, especially in the presence of their principal. So the positive and negative effects of discussions on the cohesiveness of the entire group need to be measured in the tiny increments of each and every interaction. This requires leadership. The principal's role is to splice one teacher's bold and secure statement on a sensitive topic and join it to another teacher's obvious apprehension so that both teachers will feel supported in their different but particular stage-in-career perceptions. A further leadership goal is to help the teacher facilitators of the discussions to recognize these subtleties of interpersonal dynamics and learn how to bridge that communication gap for themselves and their colleagues. The smaller group conversations have proven to be a good intermediate training ground for just that purpose.

RECONCEIVING LEADERSHIP ROLES

Roles have been redefined. Teachers are beginning to assume the role of facilitating some faculty discussions. My role, still in the making, is to listen and participate as appropriate. I am very conscious of my facial expressions and body language so as not to intrude upon any comments or discussions that may be sensitive and not usually brought by teachers to an administrator's awareness. With ambivalence, I try to resist what I know to be the most natural inclination for teachers, that is, to elicit the affirming gaze of the administrator as they are expressing a new idea or opinion. For the sake of all of us, we need to gain experience in bestowing the affirming gaze upon one another.

The stage is now set for many years of rich collaborative conversation leading toward systemic change. At every faculty meeting we gain practice in listening and responding respectfully to one another as we converse about important issues of teaching and learning and confront our samenesses and differences. The strong sense of faculty community that is nourished in our meetings tends to reinforce the understanding that each and every interaction among us is an opportunity to partake in a cherished commodity that we don't take for granted.

When the meetings end we take those refined skills back to the classroom and gather our children on the rug, better able to transform the insights we've gained in our teacher rugtime into building a positive community for our students. For all of us, we are continuing to learn how to extend these insights into our daily interactions with each other and all groups in the school—faculty, staff, custodial, secretarial, and administrative. The ripples outward from our transformed meetings have had a salutary effect on all who are involved on our school life.

RUGTIME RECONSIDERED: SLIPPING OFF THE TIGHTROPE

THAT IS HOW I ended the above article. But there's more to this story. Leaders are always learning. Let's go back to the tightrope image: "The distance between one teacher's casual remark and an entire faculty's readiness for change can be likened to a tightrope that (a principal must travel) with intention and patience." Looking back on this issue of eliminating announcements from the structure of our faculty meetings, I can see that my balancing pole was angled too heavily toward intention and not sufficiently poised with patience. That imbalance caused me to lose the security of a fully centered position and to "slip off the tightrope." I later realized that in my zeal to energize on the issues of real import, we were neglecting, to some degree, the housekeeping matters that keep a school running efficiently. Some announcements were simply too important to all of us for them to be neglected. More important, I failed to realize that the sharing of an announcement is a vehicle for a staff member to speak to the group, however briefly, and benefit from receiving colleagues' positive acknowledgment and gratitude.

SOLVING A PROBLEM NOT PERCEIVED AS A PROBLEM: A PROBLEM

I had committed a cardinal sin of leadership—I had moved too fast! Resolving a problem that is not yet perceived as a problem by others is not a good resolution. Although everyone welcomed and appreciated the need for focusing on a single topic, the elimination of announcements at the beginning of each faculty meeting hit a sore nerve.

I failed to fully realize that the very process of changing our meeting format required more time for the faculty to dwell on and consider its strengths and weaknesses. Looking back, it would have been a great topic for discussion—a missed opportunity. My impatience for "doing it a better way" caused me to shift this leadership task to a management timeline, that is, "now." That shift in my thinking resulted in my acting as a manager rather than as the leader I was striving to be.

After only a few meetings with the new format, the teachers made it clear to me that I had moved too quickly. They were not disagreeing with the idea that announcements took up too much time; rather, they took issue with my way of resolving that problem. They felt that announcements could and should be included in our meetings, but the "how" needed some attention. The issue was resolved efficiently and effectively by a small group of teachers who designed a sign-up sheet so that the time needed for announcements could be anticipated. A notice of an upcoming faculty meeting is posted along with the topic of the meeting and who will be facilitating the discussion. Space is left on the notice for teachers to enter their name and a couple of words about the subject of their announcement, for example, social committee business, welcoming a student teacher, a call for a committee, and so forth. The very act of signing up for an announcement causes each of us to pause and consider whether the announcement, however brief, is an appropriate use of the group's time or whether it can just as well be made outside the meeting via e-mail, mailbox, or the metal clip. The hunt for the long-arm stapler is still appropriately relegated to "wanted posters" in the photocopier room where it belongs.

What was needed was so simple as to be unseen. We needed a way to separate out required announcements from focused discussion on topics of mutual interest and concern. Once that was accomplished the proper balance—affirmation of shared leadership—was reestablished. As for me, it was time to climb back onto that tightrope and move onto the next project.

RELEARNING A BASIC LESSON OF LEADERSHIP

Although the meeting issue was resolved when a needed balance was better achieved, a larger issue of how and when new ideas are best raised, and who should be involved in introducing and implementing them, is embedded in that scenario and how it played itself out. New ideas are the lifeblood of a vital, growing organization. But how can they be conceived and carried out with maximum effect and minimum detriment? How do new ideas in a school setting navigate their way optimally from clear conception to widespread acceptance and effective practice?

Good ideas often have a better chance of survival if they are sponsored by someone other than the building administrator. Even when excellent relationships exist with their staff, principals are naturally regarded to some degree with a suspicious eye. It goes with the job. Teachers are apt to attribute unintended motivation to an administrative suggestion. At the risk of sounding defensive, there is some truth to the saying that "no good deed goes unpunished." In this case, "no administrator's good idea escapes suspicion."

At times, we principals misunderstand a major component of our leadership role—promoting good ideas. We don't need to author these ideas; we just need to make sure the good ones are sustained. No, let me be more clear—it is usually best for the principal not to author these ideas, at least not overtly.

ADVANCING IDEAS QUIETLY

Some advice. Listen for good ideas arising from the teachers. Whenever your sensitive antennae pick up a very promising one, acknowledge the creator of the idea: "Diane, that's a really good idea; could we put it on the agenda for our meeting?" Or, if that kind of highlighting tends to overwhelm a teacher, ask another teacher to fulfill that role on your behalf: "Tell Diane she's got a great idea and convince her that we should put it on the agenda for our meeting." The idea is acknowledged as Diane's; you've given it a gold star for inventiveness. Now step aside and let it be birthed. On a good faculty, teachers love to promote one another's ideas, especially on the principal's behalf, in hopes that the principal may be thinking about their ideas in the same positive light.

People tend to like their own ideas better than someone else's. In a collective sense, teachers consider any other teacher's idea as their own, but yours as "someone else's." Still, you can learn how to navigate these murky idea waters with good wisdom.

Never start a faculty meeting with "I want to present an idea to you that I've been thinking about." Eyes will narrow; you'll see teachers shifting in their chairs as they get ready to pick it apart in ways you could never imagine (politely, of course). If you just take the time to recast that idea into somebody's else's authorship, I promise you, it will be heard and openly considered. Not always accepted, of course, but heard and given some chance of survival. It's uncanny.

Go ahead and have your own ideas. Just don't always feel that you need to tell people they're yours. Experienced principals know there are numerous ways to feed good ideas to a group of teachers so that it seems that they themselves came up with them. (Veteran principals will have to forgive me for outing them on these techniques.) Teachers' discussions can be naturally led to uncovering a good idea you've had in mind without a sense that it came from you.

Here's some useful language for promoting ideas: "I thought I heard the third-grade team dealing with this issue a while back. [Didn't happen, but should have.] They had a terrific idea to [do something]" or "More than one of you has told me that we need to [whatever]." In fact, nobody has told you that—*you* told you that. But it's a reasonable possibility that teachers would come up with that idea so you are safe to defer to that possibility. It gets the idea out there with no burden of being imposed from above. There's mutuality in purpose when it comes to good ideas. Teachers need their principal to recognize their good ideas and to help get their ideas launched into acceptance. You need the teachers to take ownership of your ideas.

If all else fails (or time is short), grab an influential faculty member, raise the idea as something you are sure he or she has mentioned or is likely to mention, and tell her you think she's had a terrific idea and you want to help her launch it. She will be happy to oblige you. Trust me—it works. If this all sounds too manipulative and contrived, get over it. If it turns out not to be a good idea, it won't survive anyway.

This is not intended to portray teachers as uncreative consumers of somebody else's ideas. Nothing could be further from the truth. I have had the distinct pleasure of working with an extraordinarily creative and devoted group of teachers for the past two decades. They have come up with countless good ideas that I could never have imagined myself. In fact, a problem with teachers' ideas, often, is that they don't realize how good their ideas are and so they are reticent to voice them. By nature, teachers worry about being regarded as boastful or wanting to be "in charge." In addition, they often don't have the larger perspective on the school and its workings that you do, so it's hard for them to see their ideas in the larger context you can provide. These subtle aspects of teacher perception are impediments to the journey of their good idea. You can get it on the road by acknowledging your admiration for it, your gratitude for it, and your excitement about helping it come to fruition. For most teachers, your posture as a willing and powerful enabler will be gratefully accepted and respected. And the idea will have its best prospects for survival.

RUGTIME FOR TEACHERS: A TIME TO DISCUSS IDEAS

Ideas have a characteristic journey as they move from imagination to implementation. Good ideas, no matter what their source, need a principal's mentoring so that their path is cleared for takeoff. Principals exercise one of their most important leadership functions by valuing ideas, providing space and time for their expression, recognizing good ones, attributing them and encouraging them, and carefully nurturing their success. It helps to be selfless in this responsibility. The rewards, in teacher morale and school healthiness, are very great.

Of course, all of this assumes that you have at least a few teachers in place who are able to or willing to learn how to contribute to the kind of positive culture you're building. The next chapter is an in-depth exploration of the most crucial leadership task for a principal: hiring teachers. Your ability to find and select new teachers, to recognize their potential as well as support them, especially in their beginning years, will have direct and serious consequences for your success as a principal.

LEADERSHIP LESSONS

- When thinking about faculty meetings, be mindful of what precious little time you have together for refining and reinforcing the positive faculty community that is so required of a good school. Consider your role and the faculty's role in the planning of those meetings.
- The size of a staff can impede a school's sense of community. Making friends—developing a community of people who care for each other—is a need unrelated to a person's age. It is, however, a need that is more easily fulfilled in groups of modest size.
- A principal's role in defining and nurturing a productive issue for discussion at faculty meetings is first to pluck it out of the many chaotic conversations in hallways and name it as a topic of importance and mutual concern. Once designated as a topic, the principal's job is to calm people down, respond to all the misinformed rumors, and lay out a process for staff to use to uncover and discuss the many layers of concerns this topic involves.
- The distance between one teacher's casual remark and an entire faculty's readiness for change can be likened to a tightrope that a principal travels with intention and patience. A principal's job is to discern the clear path from the perception of disequilibrium to the resolution of balance without complicating the process with other issues.
- Don't commit the cardinal sin of leadership—making changes too quickly! Resolving a problem that is not yet perceived as a problem by anyone but you is not a good resolution.
- At times we principals misunderstand a major component of our leadership role—promoting good ideas. We don't need to always author these ideas: we just need to make sure the good ones are sustained. No, let me be more clear—it is usually best for the principal not to author these ideas, at least not overtly.
- All teachers do not enter a group discussion with common feelings of safety, especially in the presence of their principal. The positive and negative effects of discussions on the cohesiveness of the entire group needs to be measured in the tiny increments of each and every interaction. This requires leadership. The principal's role is to splice one teacher's bold and secure statement on a sensitive topic with another teacher's obvious apprehension so that both teachers will feel supported in their perceptions.

- A further leadership goal for the principal is to assist teacher leaders in learning how to recognize the subtle interpersonal dynamics of the faculty meetings and learn how to bridge that communication gap for themselves and their colleagues. Smaller group conversations have proven to be a good intermediate training ground for just that purpose.

Clarifying Episode:
Hiring the First Teacher

It was only days after supervising the painting the pole when I was hurled into a real leadership task—hiring a teacher, my first one as principal. A teacher stopped by the office to anxiously notify me that due to unforeseeable situations with her husband's job, their family needed to move to Ohio—next week!

It was Thursday and school began the following Wednesday. Not yet realizing that I should be at least as anxious as she was, I received her news calmly, wished her well, and then we both went down to her classroom to box up her things.

Slowly, I came to the realization of my predicament. I was just now realizing that I would be responsible for finding her replacement. Yikes! I had no sense of how one proceeds in these matters. I was bereft of any firsthand hiring experience as a principal. I frantically grabbed the phone to make a few quick calls to the superintendent and my principal colleagues. Within the hour, as a result of their leads and guidance, I had a stack of files in front of me. I called any and all names given to me. I was now networking, calling principals in the area—introducing myself and begging for any assistance in the form of, hopefully, the name of a teacher who could take this position, or at least, another name of someone to call in pursuit of that ideal. Names quickly gathered on my pink message slips. I called each name on the list. Most already had jobs. Some promised to call me back. A few sounded promising. I made appointments to meet three of these candidates.

I sought the help of another administrator to coach me in what questions to ask. This complete naïveté with something so central to the success of my school—hiring teachers—was anxiety-producing to say the least. I met with the three applicants, and it was clear to me which one I wanted. I arranged for a couple of the teachers to meet her to gauge their response. I called her references, got the okay from the superintendent, and called her back to offer her the job. She accepted!

With the help of my colleagues, and some enormous good luck, I found just the right person for this position. I was ecstatic. Before I went home that evening, I stopped in the foyer to take another look at my glistening white pole—I was already mourning the loss of simpler days.

5

Hire Teachers as If Your Professional Life Depends on It: It Does!

This is where the "rubber meets the road" with respect to a principal's leadership. Who should I hire? Which one is the best fit for this particular vacancy? Our hiring decisions are crucial to our professional effectiveness. Even if your district's central office completes all hiring and teachers are assigned to your building, a principal can still make use of an interview process within the school to serve as part of a mentoring process. The success of our leadership days depends, in large part, on our hiring decisions, each one shaped by our intuitions, our values, and our ability to see potential. Over time, if you remain as principal for an extended period, your entire staff will be a composite of what matters to you—a collective extension of how you think. Do you trust your hiring skills?

"GOT A MINUTE?"

A PHRASE that fills most principals with a queasy uneasiness and heightened anxiety, especially when uttered by a teacher in late spring or, heaven forbid, late summer—"Got a minute?" When a teacher approaches you with these casual words, you make time. It won't be a minute—and the reason for the meeting is not casual. Most principals recognize this phrase as the introduction that precedes the worrisome message, "I'm not coming back next year," or, gulp!, "I can't finish out the year." The reasons are often logical and understandable: a baby is expected, a spouse's job is relocated, family or personal illness, a far-away boyfriend, returning to school, or re-tirement. Sometimes, however, a teacher's leaving is crisis-related and calls upon other specified administrative skills intended for those occurrences.

Over the years I have engaged in quite a few normal attrition "got a minute" conversations with teachers, and I've come to recognize the similar rhythm, format, and expectations of these exchanges. A teacher appears in my doorway. Surmising my availability, and in a quiet voice, she utters the fated phrase, "Got a minute?" I say, "Sure." As I motion the teacher into my office, she eyes the door—a sure sign that a secret is about to be divulged. I close the door, maintaining a calm and easy smile for the benefit of those watching me close that door.

"I'M NOT RETURNING NEXT YEAR"

As I move piles of folders from the chairs in my office to secure some sitting space for both of us, we exchange brief comments about how our day is going and mutually lament the busyness of this time of year. There's an expected nervousness in her voice. I, too, am nervous and a bit embarrassed at my distraction, as mentally I'm going through my "good candidates file" for my first impressions of a worthy replacement. The teacher is just now getting seated, shifting the piles of folders and just-retrieved mailbox miscellany in her own arms and trying to balance a much-needed mug of coffee as well. By this time it feels like we've been in there for hours.

A pause. She looks at me intently and takes a deeper than normal breath. "I'm not coming back next year." There—it's done. Her relief in getting these few words out is palpable. Tears well up for both of us in that brief instant as we mutually catalogue the images of many good memories—our history—now coming to a close. I recognize how difficult it has been for this teacher to get to this moment. There's no second chance for a first impression in these situations, and so it's important that a principal react in a supportive man-ner when presented with this news. It's an important part of leadership.

She goes on to explain that her husband's firm has relocated him to Atlanta. We take some time to review the schooling possibilities for her chil-dren. I promise to give her the phone number of a former student's family who recently moved to that area and to make some contacts with principals there I know. My immediate attention is now on the person in front of me—to help her feel some comfort about the difficult process of moving the fam-ily to a new city and leaving a job she loves and friends she cherishes. She needs to feel appreciated, not guilty about leaving. Together we work through the sequence of necessary notifications to superintendent, school board, fac-ulty, parents, and students. I make a mental note that the designated faculty committee needs to be notified of this teacher's leaving so that the appropriate rituals can be activated.

It's natural for a principal to feel disappointed by the news (though in some cases it may be good news) that a teacher is leaving, and to not be thrilled by the extra work involved in starting up the interview process. However, much harm can be inflicted on the relationship if a principal doesn't keep upset feelings in check. My view is to make the most of and enjoy the time each teacher is with us, and I am grateful for any hours (prior to Labor Day!) that remain to consider how to fill this vacancy.

RITUALS AND TRADITIONS FOR TEACHERS LEAVING THE SCHOOL

Beginnings and endings—two significant bookends in the life of a school. A school's culture includes a wide array of carefully calibrated rituals and traditions for teachers and staff leaving the school. Elementary teachers, especially, accumulate significant amounts of wisdom about fairness and evenness from young children. They know, for example, that birthday treats need to be exactly the same, that everyone needs to be the "line leader" at least once, and that saying goodbye the right way is very important. Teachers activate this knowledge as they construct a continuum of differentiated rituals to address the many reasons for teachers leaving—a new baby, retirement, moving out of the area after 1 or 2 years versus moving after 10 years. There are sad reasons for a teacher leaving as well. Teachers leaving or retiring due to illness or a teacher whose employment has been terminated by the administration are always considered to be difficult situations. But dependable and loyal social committees include appropriate farewells for all these employees in their planning. All of these requisite decisions made by colleagues on behalf of colleagues are woven into the life fabric of the school and promote what becomes known as that staff's culture.

GET YOUR HIRING HAT ON

As the social committee plans the ending ritual or honoring celebration for a teacher who is leaving, the principal focuses on the next phase—the selection of that teacher's replacement. A frenzy of simultaneous activity seizes you, depending on the time of year. What are you looking for? Where will you find good candidates? Are you hiring for the position that teacher held, or will you switch some teacher assignments around, thus creating a vacancy at another grade level or in another position? In considering switching around, you weigh the many pros and cons of each move. What is gained by that switch? How difficult will it be to locate a replacement for the teacher who switches positions? For example, if your librarian is certified to teach third grade and would like to get back to the classroom, you may find that it's far more difficult to locate qualified candidates for that librarian vacancy than it would be to get candidates for that third-grade classroom. What do you do? There are so many layers of concerns and possibilities. A larger issue of keeping the librarian, who is a known good teacher, motivated and excited about teaching may easily overshadow your concern about finding a new librarian, and so you decide to give that third-grade to the librarian and spend those extra hours in securing a new librarian, grateful to that library teacher for being the good teacher she is. This is just one of many scenarios you will confront as you embark on the huge task of hiring.

Under ideal circumstances you will have lots of candidates to choose from and lots of time to decide. However, you rarely operate under ideal circumstances, so you need to do everything you can do to maximize your opportunity to find the best candidate for the job by approximating those ideal circumstances ahead of time. Get yourself organized by following some basic guidelines.

React in a supportive manner when teachers announce they're leaving. This begins with the "got-a-minute" conversations. How you handle the news of a teacher leaving will, in part, determine the comfort level of the staff in bringing you that all-important announcement as early as possible in the future. If you react to this news in an angry or upset manner, making the teacher feel guilty or uncomfortable, that news will travel fast through the faculty, and teachers will be reticent to share their news any earlier than they absolutely must. Reacting in a supportive manner is the right thing to do, and it may bring this news to you sooner rather than later.

Encourage staff to inform you early even if they are just considering leaving. It's helpful for a principal to know that a teacher is tentative about returning so that you can keep a good candidate in mind or stay in contact with possible candidates. Keep in mind that leaving is a difficult and complicated event for a teacher. Teachers are often reticent to tell their principal that there's even a possibility they may not be returning. The reasons are a mixture of not being sure, not wanting people to know just yet, not wanting to worry their principal, anxiety that their principal will be upset or think of them differently, and keeping their options open. Teachers are not thinking about what you need to do to fill the vacancy. That's your job. So you need to figure out ways to uncover possibilities of vacancies as early as you can.

Always anticipate the possibility of a vacancy on your staff for the coming year. Many principals wonder if they need to interview and when. The answers are "yes" and "regularly." The hiring clock doesn't start ticking when the teacher tells you she's leaving. It's always ticking, so use it to your advantage. It's best to interview candidates, at the very least by telephone, throughout the year whether you know you have a vacancy or not.

At an early January faculty meeting I make my annual announcement: "If there's anything about your life that you know that I should know, please let me know sooner rather than later—it really helps me in securing the best candidates for our consideration." The announcement helps, but it's still only January. Those who are reticent to tell you may be helped along with a simple form. In February, I put a "Thinking about next year" form in mailboxes (See figure 5.1 for an example of this form.)

I have found this simple form very helpful in encouraging early conversations about vacancies for the coming year. It serves as a reminder to teachers that you are already thinking about next year and that they should let you know if they are leaving. Teachers usually respond honestly to this memo or don't return it. If they don't, that, of course, constitutes a response.

KEEP AN EYE ON YOUR PROJECTED STUDENT ENROLLMENT

Keeping track of enrollment projections is another necessary step in anticipating your staffing plan for the following year. Vacancies are not always created by a teacher leaving. Another reason to hire a teacher is because student enrollment is growing and you need to open a new class section. Will you be able to retain all current teachers? Have you followed the district's procedures and timelines for notifying those teachers you may not be able to retain? Are they tenured/nontenured? In addition to classroom teachers, how will a rise in enrollment affect your non-classroom teaching faculty? Do you need to hire additional staff for music or physical education or special education? Alternatively, if there is a drop in enrollment, will this result in reduction of staff in these subject areas?

Keeping Track of Families Moving Out

Not unlike the teachers, families may be reticent to share information that they are considering a move out of the area. They may be uncertain about an anticipated promotion and may not want family or neighbors to know just yet. Parents are not thinking about what you need to do if enrollment rises or falls from specified levels that warrant opening or closing a section. In some cases,

FIGURE 5.1. Thinking About Next Year Memo

To: All Faculty
From: Beth
Re: Thinking about next year

    As you know, at this time of year I'm already working on our Staffing
Plan for next year. I'm in conversation with teachers on leave and non-tenured
staff who are all, understandably, trying to make plans for next year. Usually I
just ask the general question at one of our January faculty meetings, "Is there
anything about your life I should know about?" and leave it at that. I thought
I'd be a bit more deliberate again this year in asking you your plans for the
_____ school year. It'll help everyone in their planning.

Thanks!
B.

RESPONSE SHEET

Thinking ahead to the _____ school year . . .

_____ "I plan to return to Crow Island next year."

_____ "We need to talk about my plans for next year."

_____ "We've already talked about my plans for next year."

NAME: _____

Please return to Beth by February ___.

your enrollment at a particular grade level is close to your capacity (and by
the way, what *is* that number?), so one or two students will make a big difference. In those situations you may want to consider writing a letter similar to
the one in figure 5.2 to current parents, asking them whether they're planning
to re-enroll their child(ren) next year. Just as with the memo to teachers, parents usually respond honestly to the form. Again, no response is a response.

Keeping Track of Families Moving In and "Shoppers"

Throughout the year principals receive phone calls from families who are
considering or who already know they are moving into the area and have

FIGURE 5.2. Keeping Track of Enrollment Letter to Parents

Dear Parents of 3rd graders,

   I'm already well into the planning of the _____ school year. As you know, our current 3rd-grade class enrollment has grown in number over the past two years. At this time I am attempting to obtain more exact enrollment figures so I can prepare our staffing plan.

   In helping me to have a more precise idea of our 4th-grade class size, please indicate (below) your plans for next year with regard to your child's enrollment at Crow Island. I realize plans change over the summer, but it would be very helpful to know your plans as of this date.

   I appreciate your assistance with this enrollment projection.

Sincerely,
Elizabeth A. Hebert
Principal

CHILD: _____ Current teacher: _____

_____ Yes, my 3rd grader will definitely be at C.I. next year for 4th.

_____ We will be relocating next year.

_____ There is some possibility that we will be moving but presently our plans are to be at Crow Island

NAME: _____

---

children to enroll for the next school year. And some calls and requests for tours of the school come from families who may be relocating to your community. They're often labeled "shoppers." (Obviously, families move in during the current school year as well—often with very little, if any, notice. In those instances your options may be limited. Considering adding a teacher assistant to a class where enrollment is high may be preferable to hiring a new teacher and reassigning students at that grade level.) It's important to keep track of these names and contact information for move-ins and shoppers, because important staffing decisions need to be made in early spring. Although the population of shoppers may seem like the least important folks on your radar screen, I try to make time to meet with them, however briefly, when they are in the area and want to tour the school. A lot of information can be gleaned in a brief meeting that will be most helpful to you if, in fact, they do enroll their child in your school. After meeting with these shopping families, I make a few notes and keep these notes in an "in the wings" file. If they do relocate to the school's attendance area, I pull those notes out to remind myself of their visit and any impressions I had that may help me in placing their child in a particular classroom. Keeping track of these shoppers is helpful at times when the enrollment at a grade level is on the edge. You may need to consider requesting an additional section and another teacher.

A STAFFING PLAN REVIEW:
KEEPING TRACK OF CONVERSATIONS,
HOPES, AND POSSIBILITIES

It's a good idea to review your staffing plan at regular intervals for two reasons. First, you want to be sure that your staffing needs are in keeping with your enrollment projections. Alternatively, you need to be sure your staffing does not exceed your enrollment projections. Do you need to alert teachers to the possibility of not having a position for them next year? What steps do you need to follow in those cases?

Second, you should review your staffing plan regularly to keep it fresh and alive. What's a good staffing plan? I'd say it's when you have outstanding teachers assigned to positions they love and all doing a good job in those positions. That's the goal. When you're on one of those "getting to the balcony" walks around your building and you have nothing else to do (right!), think about possible vacancies and how you'd fill them. "What if Ann retires?" "Who would be good on that grade-level team?" "What if we need a part-time reading teacher?" "How would I fill that spot?" "Who's on leave and would work well in that position?"

Teachers think about this all the time on their own behalf, and so should you. Jot down notes of conversations with teachers and evaluation conference notes and slip them into your staffing plan file. "Sandy really wants 2nd grade"; "Mary Ann would really love a job-share if available"; "Bill is thinking about positions with more administrative responsibilities"; "Karen would like to be back full-time"; "Who else is out on leave, tenured or nontenured?"

Of course, you may wish to plant seeds for switching to another position in a goal conference or evaluation conference with a teacher. You may be looking for a spot that achieves a better fit for a teacher currently on staff, a good teacher, but perhaps not currently in the best position at this time.

FINDING CANDIDATES FOR VACANCIES
AND NEW POSITIONS

A significant limitation to the hiring process is the pool of candidates available to you at the particular time you are hiring. You can increase that pool by staying in touch with former student teachers, teacher assistants, and substitute teachers who worked well in the school. Hang on to résumés of candidates you were interested in a few years ago but for various reasons could not pursue at that time. Collect all of these names into a "good candidates file." You can smooth out the unevenness of candidate pools from year to year by contacting candidates from this stash.

Networking is another way to find candidates. Staying in touch with administrative colleagues in other districts can be a lifeline of possible candidates. You may feel that you're in competition with your colleagues for candidates at the same time, but remember, we're not all looking for the same kind of teacher. So staying in contact with neighboring principals can unearth many good possibilities, especially if you have been helpful when they were in need.

LOOKING AT RÉSUMÉS

Depending on your school district's size and procedures, candidates may send applications and résumés to a central office designee (such as a Superintendent or Assistant Superintendent of Personnel), directly to building principals, or to both. If your district uses a central office hiring procedure and new teachers are assigned to your school without your participation in the process, you will find some of the ideas in this chapter still relevant and useful, although in need of adjustments for your particular circumstances.

If you are involved with even preliminary staffing decisions, at some point you'll have a pile of résumés, and you'll need to pluck out from that pile some teachers you will call, some teachers you will meet, some teachers you will interview, and, hopefully, at least one teacher you will hire. In your early years as principal it's best if you can get some advice from a superintendent, personnel manager, or a fellow principal to help you with the initial sort.

Principals read a résumé in their own unique manner and devise their own reliable formulas for separating résumés into the three piles of "*no*," "*possibly*," and "*good candidates*." Ultimately, the best way of sorting résumés is the process that will yield the best candidates for *your school*— vacancy after vacancy, year after year. Now you just need to discover what that process is. As you review résumés, notice what process you are using and keep track of how effective or ineffective that process was in filling each vacancy. What do parents and teachers think of your hiring?—an important question to ask yourself. How will you find out?

At times when the candidate pool is quite large, a good résumé may easily find its ill-fated sweep into the "*no*" pile, because principals often use large organizers, (e.g., applicant has a graduate degree or at least 3 years of experience) just to get the pile down to a manageable number of résumés for consideration. Conversely, when the candidate pool is small, a resume from the potential "*no*" pile could find its way to "*possibly*." Take some time to jot down for yourself what process you're using and track its effectiveness over time.

This is not a science. These are human decisions subject to human error, but the goal is to keep the human errors to a minimum. All eyes are on your hiring decisions, so make sure your careful eyes are on it, too.

PREPARING FOR THE INTERVIEWS

Forming the Interview Committee

Many, if not most, schools or school districts form some kind of committee to interview teacher candidates. Each principal (or administrator in charge of personnel) makes decisions about how that committee is formed—its size, its makeup, its duties. Some principals may utilize an interview committee early in the process, to review résumés and make recommendations or decisions about which candidates to interview. Other principals may do the selecting themselves and then present only finalist candidates for the committee to interview.

Usually, a good committee is one that includes the perspectives of a diverse faculty community. (This committee of teachers can also serve as a useful mentoring group for meeting with those teachers who are hired by your central office and assigned to your building.) What about size? A smaller group selected by the principal has its advantages. Each member of an invited and designated group tends to take the responsibility seriously. You can ensure more uniformity in the sequence of questions and have more control of the interview. Also, meeting with a smaller group can be less stressful for the candidate.

Another alternative is to consider the interview committee as an open-ended invitation to anyone who would like to join it—no special invitees. The size is controlled only by the probability that everyone who wants to be at the interview won't be able to make the particular date. Still, everyone feels equally invited and part of the process. Of course, there are disadvantages to this open-invitation format as well. The size itself may be unwieldy for your group; the open invitation may be construed as a less serious commitment to this duty; there may be some "loose cannons" who appear at the interview and take this opportunity to vent their feelings on some issue, a scenario you may not find helpful in that you hope to impress this candidate with the better side of your staff.

Over the years, I've used both the small, select group and the large, open group approaches. I would recommend the large, open-ended invitation because it creates opportunities for a staff development focus. In February, I send an open invitation similar to the one presented in figure 5.3 to all faculty to be part of the current year's interview committee.

Scheduling and Structuring the Interviews

Putting together a schedule of interview times can be exasperating. Each school/school district has its own rules, procedures, and practices as to when

FIGURE 5.3. Interview Committee Memo to Teachers

To: All Faculty
From: Beth

Please let me know if you would like to be included on a FACULTY INTERVIEW COMMITTEE to meet candidates for vacant teaching position(s) for next year.

Thanks,
B.

RESPONSE SHEET

_____ Yes, please include me on the Faculty Interview Committee for:

    ____ Classroom Teachers

    ____ Special Subjects Teachers (Music/Art/PE/Library/Spanish)

    ____ Pupil Services Team

    ____ Non-certified staff

NAME: _____

PLEASE RETURN TO BETH BY _____ . . . thanks!

extra duty meetings can be scheduled. Beginning principals especially need to consult these regulations so that they understand the parameters of scheduling extra meetings. Trying to weave around a school district's calendar of after-school meetings and additional teaching responsibilities, as well as teachers' personal commitments, to find a time when everyone (including the candidate, of course) is available, can be maddening. Some wisdom on scheduling interviews: don't schedule it on a Friday if it can be helped. Wednesdays and Thursdays are often considered to be the best days, that is, the latter part of the week, all other things being equal. But of course, all other things are not equal and so you have to schedule it when you, the candidate, and as many of the teachers and staff as possible are able to make it.

At our school, the interview is scheduled after school at 3:45. We dismiss students at 3:15, so this gives teachers and staff time to take a breath, grab a cup of coffee, and get to the interview location. At times we've needed to interview during the school day and get classes covered with subs. That option may work well in many schools, but it doesn't work as well at ours because teachers are distracted by knowing their students are in the building. Life's not perfect. We do the best we can.

Preinterview Packets to the Committee

A couple of days before the interview I provide all committee members with equal amounts and kinds of information about each candidate and the date/time/location of their interview. I limit the preinterview packet to the résumé. There are reasons for this. I don't want to shape the interview with letters of recommendation that can easily be compared. Reference letters vary widely and may not always be helpful to a candidate's interview. I also don't include an applicant's cover letter in the teacher packet. Candidates' enthusiasm and writing skills vary in their opening message to a principal, personnel director, or superintendent. Teacher interviewers tend to be critical and are apt to be unforgiving of a phrase like, "I'm confident I will be an asset to your teaching staff," not remembering that once they, too, wanted that first job. Best to give them only the résumé so that they can focus on that information and the interview itself.

Assurances of confidentiality, where needed, must be included, and teachers need to be reminded of the wishes of a candidate to keep their interview under wraps. (See figure 5.4 for a sample preinterview packet memo.)

Teaching Demonstration/Sample Lessons: Yes or No?

A common practice in interviewing a teacher candidate is to have them teach a lesson while a principal and interview team observes. If at all possible, it's

FIGURE 5.4. Preinterview Packet Memo to Committee

To: (COMMITTEE MEMBER NAMES)
From: Beth

Please join me in meeting . . .

KATE SMITH

(KATE would be interested in either our 3rd- or 4th-grade vacancy)

Thursday, March 11

3:45

in Conference room

(Attached is her résumé. Just a confidentiality reminder . . . Please know that candidates have not notified their current employer that they are interviewing in another district.)

RESPONSE SHEET

____ Yes, I can join the group in meeting Kate on Thursday, March 11 @ 3:45.
____ Sorry, I can't make it.

NAME: _____

best to observe the candidates teaching in their own school and classroom. That observation has the most authenticity. However, this opportunity is often not possible or feasible; hence, the sample lesson is often conducted in the school where the candidate is interviewing. Teaching a sample lesson with a group of children the teacher does not know is fraught with difficulties. Context for the teacher candidate (i.e., what a teacher comes to know about each child, and the group as a whole) is absent from that sample lesson. A more significant problem with teaching demonstrations is that the observers are usually not in agreement about what comprises good teaching practice. That stems from the fact that teachers seldom observe one another's teaching and so they bring very different understandings of good teaching to that observation. Still, with all its warts, there is much to be learned from observing a teacher in a lesson, and so this method is often used (Johnson et al., 2004, p. 189).

Questions, Questions, Questions:
What Questions Will We Ask?

Now that you have a few candidates scheduled, what are you going to ask them? There are plenty of resources on this subject. Just go to the Internet and search for "interview questions" and you'll be rewarded (or burdened) with tons of resources. You may want the interview committee to take a look at some of these questions and discuss their relevance and strengths.

In composing interview questions, we have the tendency to list the issues and problems we can't seem to solve, and we reformulate them into questions for the candidate. We even feel very proud of ourselves when we formulate a good question: "*Yes*, let's ask her *that* question." For example, one question proposed for an interview was "We've been working on a six-day block schedule for 5 years now and we've discovered some problems. What's your experience with scheduling, and what thoughts and suggestions can you offer that may help us?" The candidate responds that she doesn't have any experience with a block schedule but would be interested in learning more about it. The interviewers look around at each other with "Now what?" expressions, and you're left empty. Better to think about that question ahead of time and reformat it to glean some information the candidate may have that may tell you more about her. "As a faculty, we've been talking about implementing a block schedule for years now—how about at your school? Do you have any persistent topics that never get resolved? Can you tell us about any of those conversations?"

Teachers are experts in formulating good questions for students in planning their lessons, so at first you may think that they'll ask good questions in an interview. Surprisingly, they often don't. In an interview, teachers tend to pose difficult and sometimes perplexing questions for their intended colleagues, questions that they themselves would find challenging to answer. Why is this? One obvious reason is that although they have a good idea about what they want to know about this new colleague, they don't have much experience in translating that curiosity into good questions. In addition, teachers often wish to communicate a high standard of performance to a possible colleague, so asking a hard question is their way of communicating that "this job is not easy. We are good at what we do and you had better be good."

It's usually a teacher's nature to not wish to offend or to make candidates feel in any way uncomfortable. Still, unstated issues of self-interest often lurk beneath their questions and comments. They experience the ambivalent feelings of wanting to be helpful and welcoming to possible new team members, but also hoping that new colleagues will be substantially self-sufficient and not require overwhelming attention from them. Will they be good colleagues? Will they be competitive with the team? Will they distinguish themselves from us, with a particular favorite teaching unit or a time-consuming weekly newsletter to parents in hopes of gaining praise from principal or parents? What will they need from me? How much of my time will need to be devoted to mentoring? Will they be a burden to the team? Can we trust this new teacher? For all these reasons, teachers are understandably nervous about their participation in an interview for future colleagues.

Really, it's the candidate's answers to questions that matter more than the questions themselves. So why not consider giving the questions to candidates ahead of time? For those who will say we need to see a candidate's immediate responses, I'd counter that there's plenty of time in an interview to assess the candidate's ability to be spontaneous. It's far more valuable toward predicting how candidates will fare in your school if you hear them present their thinking on issues or questions they've had some time to think about and to consider their responses.

Day of the Interview

I arrange for each candidate to spend the full day or at least an afternoon with us. The schedule will include touring the building, meeting faculty and staff, spending time in classrooms observing, conversations with me, time for informal chats with teachers, a preinterview meeting with me, and, finally, the group interview with the teachers.

The Preinterview Conversation: Principal and Candidate

Before the interview with the team of teachers, I sit down with the candidate and preview the interview format and questions. It helps them to relax and feel supported. Many have told me subsequently that it doesn't feel like a typical interview. In this session, I aim for a good informal conversation allowing me to get to know the candidate in a more natural setting. By establishing this meeting as a noninterview, just getting ready for the interview, you have an opportunity to work with the candidate in preparing them for the next step. The "working with" is, in fact, what you hope to do with teachers as a normal aspect of your ongoing relationship with them. So this conversation gives the principal a valuable perspective in seeing how a candidate works with you in a problem-solving situation, in this case, the upcoming interview.

You find out a lot in these conversations. I often ask candidates to practice with me so they can collect their thoughts for their interview with the teachers. I have the opportunity to hear what first comes to their mind and, in addition, the questions they have for me or for the teachers. I'm not looking for the right answer or, sometimes, even a good answer. What I'm really looking for is the capacity to form relationships, character, potential to connect with staff, and the likelihood that this person can be influenced by this school and its faculty, students, principal, parents, and community. I'm assessing how I feel when I'm interacting with this candidate, and at the same time projecting how this person will fit within our staff culture.

The Interview with Teachers—Often-Asked Questions

I move the candidate into the staff lounge for a much-needed break while I meet briefly with the interview team now gathered in an adjacent conference room to review the structure of the interview.

We usually spend a little over an hour with each candidate. Here are the often-asked questions that are basic to our interviews, together with some annotation that reminds us why we are asking that question:

"Who are you?" The interviewing teachers are anxious for this first glimpse of this possible colleague in the formal interview. Who is she? What's my first impression? Can she string words together? Am I at ease with her? After everyone's been introduced, I'll start by asking the candidate to "walk us through your résumé." This first nonchallenging question gives both the candidate and the committee time to work through the initial, and understandable, nervousness. It offers the candidate an opportunity to experience the gift of some smiles and head nods from the interviewers.

The expected response to this introductory question is a brief 2- to 3-minute statement—not a whole life. What do candidates choose to highlight? How do they read the group? Does it sound natural? It gives the teachers a chance to hear the interviewee for the first time, establish a listening rapport, and perhaps identify with something the candidate says. This question gets the rhythm and energy going for the interview.

"You mentioned [something]. That's interesting . . . tell us more about that." Something in the candidate's résumé or remarks may be particularly interesting. I'll let the candidate know that either I or one of the teachers will ask about it. I encourage the interview team to inject some personal connection. "I was interested in your experiences with social service and juvenile work. Karen and Eve have had some experience with that organization, too." This response gives the team the opportunity to hear the candidate talk knowingly about some unique experience they've noted on their résumé.

"How would your students/colleagues/administrator/parents describe you?" We're not able to interview all the many people who truly know this candidate. We're interested in knowing how a candidate thinks they are perceived by students, colleagues, administrators, and parents.

The response is a mixture of hoped-for impressions and honest self-appraisal—all very important information to be considered in an interview. Does he know himself? Is she realistically aware of how she is perceived by others?

"Describe your classroom—a recent good lesson—a typical day." This question gets at the heart of this issue—the teaching. Describing the environment, a particular child, how they organize an instructional day or a particular lesson: this is information that teacher interviewers can closely relate to, leading them on to ask more probing questions.

"Tell us about a student who is on your mind." Teacher interviewers are very interested in hearing a colleague talk about a student "on your mind." Candidates are understandably cautious when forming a response to this question. However, if they know the question is coming, they can make some judgments about what student scenario feels appropriate. It's this kind of judgment—not the specifics of the story—that a principal is interested in observing. What kind of judgment does this teacher have? On the other hand, teachers are listening for stories they can relate to—a student concern that balances vulnerability and capability.

"What do you do when you're not teaching? What makes you laugh?" Mindful to not take a detour into personal issues or other probing questions clearly inappropriate for interviews, you're trying to get an idea of the candidate's interests and sense of humor. A recent *Chicago Tribune* article on the topic of interviewing offered this possible question: "What makes you laugh?" (Kleiman, 2004). We often use that question. For any healthy community, the sharing of laughter is an essential ingredient. Does this candidate blend in with the faculty's style of humor?

"What do you need from principal/colleagues to be a successful teacher? This is a difficult question for a candidate because they are, understandably, not anxious to present themselves as in any way needful. A question like this, however, gives the team an opportunity to see if the candidate is someone comfortable enough with themselves to not present themselves as a loner or a know-it-all; can they evidence some level of vulnerability?

INTERVIEWING AS STAFF DEVELOPMENT

"What do you want to know about us?"

Before we ask our last question, I introduce this turnaround question: "We've asked you a lot of questions this afternoon; what questions do you have for us?" During the preinterview a candidate often asks me questions that are best answered in the interview and addressed to the teachers. At that time I help the candidate sort out those questions, and I encourage her to ask these questions of the teachers. It helps the candidate to relax if they feel that you are their advocate in this interview process. What I'm hoping to accomplish is to shift the vulnerability and loss of control from candidate to interviewers. It's a humbling experience to go through an interview, and so it feels more natural if we're all in the candidate's shoes for at least part of our time together. By giving the candidate some control, you give yourself an opportunity to watch her in control. How does she handle it? At the same time, you have the chance to listen to the teachers' responses.

Here's where the interview can become an outstanding opportunity for staff development. Hiring is a time-consuming project. The stakes are high; our confidence wavers as we consider the ever-varying strengths of the candidate pool from year to year. The last thing we want to do is spend hours and hours in search of a candidate that do not yield a successful hire. Instead of thinking of this as wasted hours, consider incorporating these interviews into your program of staff development. Sound crazy? It's not. In fact, the interview process (whether you hire the candidate or not) can serve as an outstanding authentic opportunity for current teachers to come together and share their beliefs and current teaching practice, have a conversation with colleagues that we never find the time to have—and share in the excitement and anticipation of a new colleague. These conversations serve as an internal audit of sorts that allows the principal to hear teachers think out loud—what matters to them?

We have precious little time to come together as a staff to hear one anothers' thoughts. It's important to capitalize on the time spent in an interview as an opportunity for teachers to practice talking to one another—to hear one another's perspectives in the authentic setting of interviewing a new teacher. "I really liked her answer to that question," one teacher says, or, "Hmm, I don't agree with what she just said," muses her colleague.

Is one grade level team of teachers responding honestly to that question about how they work together as a team? Does the candidate sense that she's being "snowed" a bit with their response? And what does she do? Leave it alone? Ask a further clarifying question? If she does, is that considered too bold by the teachers? And what did the other grade level team make of their colleagues' response to that question about team meetings? Would they have answered it in the same way? One brave teacher speaks up by saying, "Actually, our team works a little differently—we meet at least once a week to go over curriculum and the week's lessons in some detail." And now the other team of teachers hears this clear difference for the first time. These kinds of exchanges form the strong foundation for good staff development conversations. Underneath each question and response, if you listen carefully, you'll hear the barely audible chorus of "Does she fit?" "What will she be like to work with?"

The irony in framing the interview as staff development is that the interview questions asked of the candidate take on less importance and urgency. What's significant in this format is the questions the candidate has for us. Here are some questions that candidates have posed to the interview team and that have yielded some wonderful discussions at the interview:

- "I understand you have grade-level meetings in the building and in the district. How do they work?"
- "What's it like to work for your principal?"
- "What about the parents? What are their expectations of the teachers?"
- "What's important or special about your school?"
- "How do you prepare students for state testing?"
- "I understand your contract is up this year and that you're going through teacher negotiations with your school board. How's it going?"
- "What are you looking for in a team member?"
- "How does your mentoring program work? What kind of support will I receive?"

"What haven't we asked you that you'd like us to know about you?" This is usually our final question. I have prearranged the signal to the candidate that when this question is asked, the interview is coming to a close.

AFTER THE INTERVIEW

At the conclusion of the interview (and the candidate knows this in advance), I accompany the candidate out of the room for 5 minutes or so of general wrapping-up of the day, to thank her for coming, and to give her an idea of when and how she'll hear from me and the next steps in our process. Then I return to meet with the teachers for another 15 to 20 minutes. That brief time when I am out of the room is precious faculty time when teachers honestly share their unedited opinions with one another. As I'm reentering the conference room after saying goodbye to the candidate, I hear their level of engagement. In fact, it's those first 30 seconds of returning into the room that are critical to me in discerning their feelings about a candidate.

I engage the interview team in a brief exchange. I ask for impressions. As I listen, I need to be mindful of what these people's day has been like. Each interview has a palpable energy—but an energy that is fragile and susceptible to a multitude of both relevant and irrelevant factors: the weather, what happened today that may have distracted these teachers, an evening event at which they're presenting. Did this candidate present herself as possibly too strong or too weak a personality for someone on the team? A principal must be able to decode the dynamics of the interview. The team may love this candidate, but it's hot and they just want to go home to some air conditioning. One teacher is openly critical of the candidate. What does that mean? Did she feel a little threatened by her obvious competence? Teachers may be distracted by other events. Another teacher is quiet; I know she's ruminating about a difficult parent phone call earlier today. A colleague casts a glance her way across the table—she's wondering if her colleague's distraction is a lack of enthusiasm for the candidate. Now she is questioning her own feelings about this candidate. And now who's looking at *her* and reconsidering *her* intuitions? All of this happens in a matter of seconds.

There are so many layers of overt and covert meanings. I listen, watch, take in the feedback, and sort it all out later. I share with the team my overall impressions of the candidate but emphasize that there will be no final decision now. We do not vote. Once all the candidates are interviewed, I will make the decision as to whether a candidate will be recommended to the superintendent and school board.

WHO WILL YOU CHOOSE?

You've completed the interviews and now you need to make some decisions. The hiring process draws you into a three-bears dilemma of finding who is "just right" for that particular vacancy or as close to just right as you can get.

Composing a team, or a department, or a complete faculty of teachers who are comfortable with one another and can share ideas openly is a key component in creating a spirit that works cooperatively toward good teaching and hence a good school. Careful attention to a balance of diversity in age, teaching experience, life experience, gender, and ethnicity on each grade-level team can be a crucial factor in establishing the day-to-day exchanges and planning of instruction. The presence of a brand-new teacher or one with only 1 or 2 years of experience can be a very positive force on the team. Less experienced teachers naturally elicit wisdom and good ideas from their elder mentors, causing the more experienced teachers to explain what they do, at the same time hearing this explanation for themselves and, hopefully, judging the efficacy of their teaching practice.

Having all senior members on a team creates a different dynamic. You might predict that consolidating a wealth of experience and good teaching into a single grade-level team would elicit rich conversations that are not burdened by taking time out for explanations to a newer and younger colleague. It doesn't always work out that way. Experienced teachers tend to respect one another's different teaching skills and styles, at the same time fully knowing they are not equally effective. Senior teachers are far less likely to suggest improvements to each other—that's the sole job of the principal.

In my experience an important, but not sole, predictor of a teacher's success has been his/her interpersonal abilities to secure the positive mentoring, support, and encouragement from colleagues that is so needed on a daily basis. So why not have the teachers make the final decision of who is hired? Because teachers don't always know what they need despite their seeming clarity on such issues. One bad hiring decision made by teachers can have a debilitating effect on their confidence. Best to retain the final decision for the principal. As you observe the candidate both in and out of the interview, you'll be a better judge of the degree of the teachers' enthusiasm for this candidate and what qualities this candidate can bring to the group. The principal alone is in a position to view the larger context, that is, what's needed in this particular position, and what's underneath the teachers' responses.

HIRING TEACHERS—A SERIOUS BUSINESS

Before you make that final recommendation, however, let's go back in time to sorting through that pile of résumés. Let's remember how these candidates came to be selected for the interview in the first place.

Beyond the basics of seeking a qualified candidate for the job, a résumé speaks to you on a more personal level. What mattered to you as you looked at that résumé? Was it the college he went to, or his GPA? Does this candidate seem too young for the particular team you're adding to? Was she from a part of the country that you're from? What about that university—set bells off for you? Why? What about those letters of recommendation—strong enough?

What about the cover letter? Did the letter feel personal to you? Did the style of this letter remind you of someone you hired a while back and was an excellent or a poor choice? Did it sound too eager? Is that spelling error forgivable or not? Heavens, why didn't someone tell her not to use a "happy face" with her signature!

Over time you gain some familiarity with the kind of résumé that attracts you. A principal's examination of a pile of résumés takes you into the land of who *you* are. Our decisions are shaped by our personal history and our intuitions—not all of them conscious, but nevertheless implicated in our leadership in both human and professional ways.

How you think (i.e., your idiosyncrasies, your likes and dislikes, your preferences and prejudices, your intuitions) will be concretized into a gathering of people who reflect the values, instincts, and imagination that you relied on when you first glanced at their résumés.

You'll discover the frustrating disconnect between a résumé and an interview (i.e., on paper the candidate looked very promising; however, the interview was weak and far less than expected). Alternatively, taking a closer look at a résumé from your "*possible*" or even your "*no*" piles and taking a risk because of a particular experience they had or the way they express themselves that draws you to them can sometimes result in an interview that surpasses your expectation, and you may end up hiring that candidate.

WHEN IT DOESN'T WORK OUT

Obviously, there are times when a hiring does not work out as one would have hoped. It becomes clear that, for a variety of possible reasons, a teacher must be let go. You are likely to arrive at this difficult decision to terminate based on an accumulating weight of evidence that this is the only appropriate course available.

In these instances a principal needs to initiate the process for nonrenewal of a teacher's contract following an unsuccessful year or years. This is an uncomfortable, even painful, dilemma for all involved: teacher, principal, colleagues, and parents. We are charged with the responsibility of helping teachers to be successful in their teaching. At the same time, we need to recognize when the particulars of this situation—whatever they may be—resist those efforts, and therefore we need to prepare a teacher for the disappointing news that she will not be returning the following year. This process needs to be handled in a timely manner, with sensitivity, and in a way that allows the teacher to maintain dignity. Timing is crucial. It is one set of circumstances to nonrenew a first-year teacher. It is an entirely different experience to nonrenew a teacher after 3 or more years when that teacher has become part of the family of your school, or when that teacher has gained tenured status. You recognize that it's hard on the culture of the building to form a relationship with a colleague and then disconnect when things don't go well. We can't be omniscient in our hiring, but we can realize the seriousness and significance of each and every hiring decision we make.

Obviously, principals are complying with the district-sanctioned evaluation process with its requisite observations and conferences with the teacher. Still, be mindful that a teacher may not discern that the legal language of your written evaluation is a preliminary step to a nonrenewal, and will need clear language to fully grasp their unfortunate professional situation. You are now faced with the difficult problem of finding the language—the right words—for beginning that conversation with the teacher, an anguish-filled dilemma, especially for the less experienced principal.

A later stage of nonrenewal, i.e., a teacher who is about to be tenured or may already be tenured, is a unique circumstance. The language and rationale presented both orally and in writing needs to be carefully selected, probably in consultation with the school district's attorneys.

For those of you who think that hiring teachers is an annual task, the mistakes of which can be corrected at the end of each year, consider this: each teacher you hire could be on the faculty for as many as 40 years and may determine in part the future course of your school for decades to come. Consider each new teacher as to whether he/she will be an invaluable facet in the diamond of your school for at least the next 40 years. This is serious business. You must take it seriously.

WE REMEMBER OUR TEACHERS

On the occasion of our school's 50th anniversary we wrote to thousands of former students to ask them what they remembered about their elementary school years. These children's memories of school were filled with recollections of friendships, absence of friendships, loneliness on the playground, and many stories about teachers who knew them well and liked them, and teachers who didn't like them.

No one mentioned a math curriculum. No one mentioned any particular group assessment we administered. No one mentioned a phonics lesson. The memories of these 1940s children were about playground events, singing songs at special times, the crises of World War II, and particularly the memorable adults who were such an important part of their school lives. These children remembered their teachers.

As we seek to nourish an atmosphere in which lasting human values are pursued as a central school aim, we must place the hiring of exceptional teachers at the center of our responsibilities. Our professional lives, and the lives of all our students, are more dependent on this aspect of our leadership than on any other.

LEADERSHIP LESSONS

- Always anticipate the possibility of a vacancy on your staff for the coming year.

- Encourage staff to inform you early that they may be leaving, and react in a supportive manner when they make that announcement.
- Keep an eye on your projected student enrollment, including move-outs, move-ins, and shoppers.
- Review your current and projected staffing plan—keep track of conversations, hopes, and possibilities for changing assignments for current teachers and bringing new teachers on to the faculty.
- Organize your system for finding candidates for vacancies and new positions.
- Be aware of what you notice in reviewing a résumé—what matters to you?
- Even if your school system uses a centralized hiring process and teachers are assigned to your building, a principal can still utilize an adapted interview process within the school that serves as part of a mentoring program.
- Preparing for interviewing candidates is a complex task, including reviewing résumés, forming the interview committee, scheduling and structuring the interviews, compiling preinterview packets for the committee, arranging for sample lessons, finalizing interview questions, and, ultimately, hiring the successful candidate.
- Consider interviewing as an opportunity for staff development, that is, a time for members of your faculty to come together and share their beliefs and current teaching practice, and have a conversation with colleagues that we seldom find the time to have.

Clarifying Episode:
About Being a Victim

November 8, 1999

Dear Staff,

Have you ever been the victim of theft? I have. Last Wednesday morning I entered the garage under my condo to find the passenger window of my car smashed. Two cell phones, my raincoat, and a yet-to-be-used umbrella were stolen. I was one of four unit owners whose cars were "visited" during the night. As the usual early-morning crowd of us assembled in the garage, we comforted each other by exchanging lists of stolen items, each assuring the other that all of these items could be replaced for minimal cost. As we swept up the shattered glass, we were all feeling fortunate that none of us was hurt and the damage was manageable. But as we hurriedly attended to what needed to be done before we left for our busy workdays, we were all thinking the same distressing thought, ". . . but they took my things."

Upon arriving at school late that morning, I found myself, quite unintentionally, in many conversations with children about lost Pokémon cards and other missing treasures. One child whose cards were lost 2 weeks ago was still quite troubled by the event. These exchanges are certainly not new to me, but I will tell you that I listened differently that day. And maybe for the first time I heard what these boys and girls were really reporting to me without knowing it. The lost possessions are often able to be replaced, but the feelings attendant to being a victim linger.

When a child tells us that "someone took my things," let's all of us elevate that report to our priority list of issues that must be attended to with thoughtful regard for the real lost possession, i.e., feelings of safety.

Thanks for listening,

B.

6

"He Stole My Snow": Moral Dimensions of Leadership on the Playground

---

Do you remember being teased on the playground or on the way home from school? I do. I recall few of the specifics, but I have a visceral memory of how I felt in those brief moments—threatened and bewildered. The following disciplinary vignette about stealing snow may be considered small, or even trivial, in the current reality of a safe school's mind-set. And it's for that specific reason that I share it with my colleagues. The tiny seeds of moral behavior are often found in these seemingly inconsequential playground scenarios that have now become well hidden from our view by an increasing number of serious and possibly even life-threatening incidents. However, these small incidents provide us with powerful options and opportunities to use them as lessons for introducing and rehearsing the skills needed to reinforce emotional safety in our schools.

THE INCIDENT: "HE STOLE MY SNOW"

THOSE ARE the exact words he used. Sobbing inconsolably, this booted and mittened, red-cheeked seven-year-old clumped over to me on the far side of the playground. "He stole my snow!" he cried. As Charlie stood next to me, a victim of snow theft, I had a pretty good idea of what had happened without further details. Suppressing an urge to laugh at his delightfully worded complaint, I said, "C'mon Charlie. Let's go over there and see what we can do."

Snow is a big deal to schoolchildren in the Midwest. Our schools have elaborate sets of rules and guidelines for snow—regulations for snowballs, specifics of what kinds of sleds can be used, requirements that snow pants and boots be worn, procedures for hanging snow pants on the locker door and leaving wet boots outside the locker, reminders to stomp your snow boots onto the rug as you enter school so the hallways stay dry. The list goes on.

Our school is adjacent to a wooded area, an absolutely majestic winter setting that has enchanted children for decades. Everybody at our school knows what good packing snow is—it has just the right balance of water and flake so that it easily molds into a ball or a variety of snow monuments. On those special wintry days, following a heavy snowfall, children's creativity soars as they invent snow games and build snow structures to make the most of this temporary gift of the weather.

THE BACKGROUND INFORMATION

Probably since the 1940s, when the school opened, the gathering of sticks and branches to make snow forts in the woods has been considered to be one of the most loved winter activities by all the children, but on this particular day, especially by my second-grade boys. Transporting the snow from the drifts on the playground to the construction site of the proposed fort takes some know-how. Boys exert extensive energy loading saucerlike sleds or piling snow on flat toboggans or simply pushing the snow with hands, arms, and bodies over to the location of the new fort. Accumulating your building materials in this highly physical manner, it's no wonder that these boys have a strong sense of snow ownership. I moved it—so it's *my* snow.

Every once in a while, a boy may be tempted to conserve his energies by taking some snow from a neighboring fort-builder. This presents a problem. Children are simultaneously envious of this boy's devious way of obtaining snow but also incensed by this act of bullying. Once a child is discovered to be "borrowing snow without permission," that offender is often pummeled with snowballs by the victimized fort-builder and his friends. Further retaliation may result in the borrower's fort being destroyed. That act is sure to fire off a chain of fort demolitions. And then the whole process begins again.

THE INVESTIGATION

As Charlie and I crossed the playground into the woods, the expected scattering of fort-builders occurred. Eyeing my presence and suspecting my mission, they decided the best course of action was to flee. Even if they're without blame, the principal may ask them questions that cause them to betray a confidence—something to be avoided at all costs because it breaks a code that children follow unquestioningly, that you don't tell. Charlie, although a little younger and less sophisticated than many of these boys, indicated some awareness of transgressing the code. As we walked toward the woods, the expression on his face changed as he began to rethink the wisdom of reporting this incident to the principal and its subsequent effect on his social standing.

I gathered a group of boys I'll describe as "those who know" at the edge of the woods. I asked the boys to relate to me what happened starting with the word "I," that is, don't tell me what others did—tell me what *you* did. The boys are familiar with this process I use to get information about instances of bullying or other transgressions of school rules. In the usual fashion, each boy related the recollected events in a light most favorable to himself. "I thought it was extra snow." "I didn't know it was Charlie's snow." "I was trying to help Charlie get his snow back." "I didn't see anything." I was unsure at that moment whether this meeting was deepening their understanding of the effect of an unkind act on their still fragile concept of trust, or whether I was providing them with more practice in clever concealment and manipulation of the truth when relating to an adult. Principals hope for the former outcome, but are mindful of the latter.

I could see Charlie making eye contact and conspiratorial, silly expressions with some of these friends as he slowly moved away from my side to stand closer to the boys. This signaled to me that the incident was no longer an issue for Charlie. Although very upsetting at first, these boys' explanations seemed satisfactory to him at this moment, and he was now more anxious about using up more recess time in talking about it than he was about further discussion and consequences for the snow thieves.

DECIDING THE CONSEQUENCE

This is that crucial juncture when a principal has to decide what course of action to take. In that instant, and it's only seconds, you make a judgment of what, if anything, you should do. Focusing on that narrow ground between overreaction and nonresponsiveness, you read the children's faces, assess the damage, and quickly compare the dynamics of this incident with other situations involving students at this grade level. You try to recall what action you took in the past, if any. You eye the group closely and try to recall any past bullying behavior of these boys. And then you render your decision.

"So, what have we learned here, boys?" I asked. They were grateful for this question that signaled to them that our conversation was coming to a close. I saw these thoughts flashing in their minds—"Charlie's not crying—he seems okay." "I don't think our parents will be called." "Looks like she's not going to take recess away from any of us." In hopes that they were only a moment away from more fort-building, they happily parroted just the right tone of reflection and apology that principals love to hear. "Well, we learned we sure won't be taking anyone's snow." "We're sorry, Charlie." "It doesn't feel good when someone takes something from you." "I think we learned there's enough snow out here on the playground for all of us." This review of what was learned from the event serves a useful community purpose. The boys' reflective comments (however insincere at the moment) reinforce each child's knowledge that they share a common ground of moral behavior that, if not always followed, is at least acknowledged as a mutual goal.

REMEMBERING THE PURPOSE OF A DISCIPLINARY RESPONSE

It's important for principals and teachers to recognize our leadership role in providing this key element of a child's safety, that is, sharing a moral perspective. In that brief instant of comparing a situation with prior disciplinary events, principals and teachers are apt to overfocus on the particulars of the penalty and lose sight of the overarching purpose of the disciplinary act, which is to reintegrate the wrongdoers into the community of students (Goodman & Lesnick, 2001). Our first impulse is to remove a misbehaving child from the situation as a consequence and/or punishment. In some instances that may be the best and most appropriate course to follow. We need to be mindful, however, that removing a child may actually be the opposite of what that child needs to experience at that moment in order to gain or regain appropriate group skills and a positive identity within the student community.

For my "snow bullies" I decided not to remove them from the recess so that they and Charlie could gain more practice in their interactions on the playground under my watchful eye and immediately following on the heels of their own assessment of the situation. Although this instance of snow theft is tiny in the constellation of disciplinary events, it is these manageable and instructive principal–student interactions—especially for a new principal—that serve as an insightful glimpse into the social–emotional landscape of the playground.

CONVERSATIONS ABOUT FEELING SAFE: USING LEADERSHIP TO CREATE AND SUSTAIN A SAFE SCHOOL

Beyond issues of compliance with rules and schoolwide policies, how does a principal use leadership to create and sustain a safe and humane learning environment? How does the safeguarding dimension of leadership develop? Each day principals model their moral stance about behavior in how they deal with issues of misbehavior. Our stance is shaped by the communities we serve, the policies and guidelines developed by our school district, and the realities of behaviors that quite regularly transgress those codes established by that community and school. On a more personal level, however, our moral stance is shaped by who we are—our own experience or lack of experience with children's moral dilemmas, and our comfort level in dealing within the framework of the disciplinary function of our jobs.

Young children, especially, are apt to be far less influenced by a school district's written code of conduct than they are by a conversation with an adult whom they view as personally invested in their safety and moral development. Conversations between principal and child, child and child, and teacher and child are opportunities for all of us to further our commitment to a safe school environment. In addition, children need to have opportunities to hear other children talk about problem behaviors as they strive to understand their own approximations of understanding about one another's moral behaviors. And, of course, a classroom teacher's devotion to maintaining safe and respectful conduct at all times is essential. Principals need to encourage teachers to establish ongoing conversations in their classrooms about issues that are so important to the emotional lives of children.

PRINCIPALS LISTENING TO CHILDREN

If stealing snow was the most serious disciplinary incident I had to deal with in my career I would consider myself quite lucky. Of course, it hasn't been. There have been plenty of instances when a child's forgiving reaction to being bullied on the playground, such as Charlie's, was not sufficient to influence my decision about disciplinary consequences. Behaviors are sometimes significantly problematic to warrant serious interventions. A schoolwide/districtwide discipline policy is referenced in these instances.

However, for day-to-day transgressions principals create their own continuum of disciplinary actions with intermediate steps that usually include reminders to the child(ren) to not do that again, or sitting-out time for a child, or having the child write a letter of apology to the aggrieved party, or a letter to his/her parents to explain what happened. A good conversation with children exploring what's going on in their lives often serves to guide principals in meting out appropriate consequences. More serious incidents may require a principal to call parents, to meet with parents and child, to consider suspension or expulsion, or to notify and involve police juvenile officers. Hopefully, the very serious incidents will be few, and for the most part you try to match the "time with the crime." As principals develop that continuum of consequences, however, we need to be mindful of that fundamental goal of any disciplinary response, which is not to systematically mete out punishments for wrongful acts, but rather to reintegrate the wrongdoers into the community of the school and its values by having them internalize and approve both of the consequences of their unfortunate behaviors and the benefits of not repeating them.

In support of that objective, principals can't settle for rules and regulations as the sole basis for their relationship with students under the assumption that a codified morality will have anything more than a superficial impact on a child's development. More is needed of you. Principals have to assume the role of social anthropologist. You need to know how children of different ages think—what their normal behavior looks like, and how they are likely to react to ethically complex situations. New principals especially need to listen to the language of children that signals their level of conceptual understanding. A principal's credibility hinges on acknowledgment of these important age differences. Talking to a 1st grader is very different from talking to a 5th grader. If you ask a fifth grader whom you were reprimanding for hitting a classmate to "remember how our rabbit felt when some of the boys and girls poked at him?" he may wonder what planet you're from. In that same vein, a kindergartener would be bewildered by the more urgent, "You have one minute to tell me exactly what *you* did out there. And I mean the truth."

Beyond that developmental knowledge, the principal needs to know individual children and their unique reactions and dispositions. Who are the leaders? Who are the followers? Who or what is the source of energy for a string of bullying acts on the playground?

Being in the know about your students' behaviors, their growing but often faulty sense of what is acceptable and what is not, allows your interventions, when needed, to be more than keeper of the rules. A principal is obligated to serve as a wise moral leader in the eyes of the children (and for teachers and parents as well), and that expected role requires imagination, empathy, and deeply grounded developmental insight.

In readying children to talk about truly serious issues, it's a good idea to involve them in practice runs about smaller incidents like stealing snow. Engaging young children in conversation about values as specifically related to actual events or experiences helps them to understand both the positive and negative effects of their behavior, aiding them to become internally ethical rather than simply following rules as a way to avoid punishment. With this continued guidance, students begin to construct the scaffolding of their own moral behavior and beliefs.

CHILDREN LISTENING TO CHILDREN

In addition to being a member of a classroom grouping, students also recognize the importance of their associations in the larger units of the school community, that is, a grade level, a hallway of classrooms, and the entire school. Issues arise in children's daily interactions that go beyond the classroom, and children are genuinely interested in knowing what's going on in other parts of the school. They are particularly interested in asking for the rationale behind certain rules and hearing about problems that occur when those rules are not followed. Access to these conversations helps young children gauge how safe they feel and how much they feel they must know about the rules of the school.

At Crow Island School, our weekly student meetings provide this opportunity for children. Each Monday at lunchtime approximately fifty students gather in the auditorium to be a part of this open meeting, run by students. A faculty member, Mr. Martin, has served as faithful sponsor and scribe for this group for many years. The children bring their brown bag lunches and secure a seat on one of the benches in the auditorium. Four students, one each from grade levels 1 through 4, sit on the front riser facing the audience. Their names were drawn out of a box minutes before the start of the meeting. Their role in today's meeting is to be a "student leader"—to listen to their peers and offer information or comments that may assist in furthering an understanding or possibly solving an issue. A "clock person" is also selected by drawing a name out of a box. That student's job is to judge when the student audience is getting too noisy for everyone to hear the meeting, to notify the audience of children when that occurs, and to calculate how many minutes to subtract from the allotted 30 minutes as a consequence of disrupting the meeting.

When the meeting begins, students from the audience line up to voice their concerns and issues at an open microphone. As they relate a concern, they are able to gauge audience interest in their specific issue. "Some 4th graders kicked our ball onto the roof." "We want to raise money for a pop machine for kids." "There isn't enough chocolate milk at lunch." "Why don't kindergartners stay for lunch?" "Our class would like to raise money for an endangered species." "Why is the floor slanted in the auditorium?" These are among the issues and comments that cover the spectrum of concerns voiced by children ages 6 to 10.

A student new to the school approaches the microphone and asks this question of the panel of student representatives: "How come we can't throw snowballs?" The selected student leaders nod their heads, consider the issue before them, and offer their advice and wisdom. ChrisJon is today's first-grade representative. He holds the microphone with both hands and responds, "I don't think people like to be hit in the face with a snowball." He passes the microphone to the second-grader seated next to him. She nods in agreement with ChrisJon's advice and offers further information: "We can throw snowballs as long as the red flag is up. When the snow is just right and deep you can throw snowballs as long as the red flag is up." Samantha is in third grade, and she further clarifies the meaning of "safe snow": "The PE teachers go out in the morning and check for ice and pebbles in the snow and if there isn't any they put the red flag up and then you can throw snowballs." Louise offers the final comments with the well-earned authority of a fourth-grader. "Basically you can only throw snowballs on the back playground and only when the PE teachers have posted the red flag. The red flag means that the snow is soft, but also it is good for packing" (Martin, n. d.). The new student who asked the question listens carefully to this information in terms that can only be provided by students. Teachers don't own this kind of valuable information. Of course they know about no snowballs and the red flag. But the PE teachers going out to check for ice and pebbles? Only kids have that kind of intelligence—and imagination!

Student meetings are just one symbol of a school devoted to children's issues. At these gatherings, children can hear other children and begin to develop their own opinions about matters of mutual concern. Not all of these issues can be resolved, but students experience a shared forum where they can access the thinking of older/younger students in readiness for the kind of exchange of opinion that will be required of them in future years.

TEACHERS LISTENING TO CHILDREN

Children present complaints and issues to teachers each and every day. Teachers are overwhelmed with juggling the schedule of each day, and they struggle to find the time to accommodate these often lengthy conversations about problematic episodes on the playground or in the lunchroom. Teachers wish they had that time, but schools in our culture have placed highest priority on curriculum, schedule, and test scores, imposing significant limitations on teachers' discretionary time to attend to students' expressions of moral/ethical issues. We need to reexamine the values that impede a teacher's ability to hear a child in the act of forming habits of moral behavior.

The importance of classroom teachers attributing significance to discussions about behavior, and their commitment to maintaining the emotional safety of the students, is fundamental to any program that seeks to assist children in formulating an understanding of the complexities of their own moral behavior. In addition to the obvious need for rules of behavior and discipline that will ensure feelings of safety, children also require credible and identifiable routines and forums for resolving disputes and solving problems relevant to their lives. In this regard, teachers in our school set aside a designated time for classroom meetings, or rugtimes, that serve as a time to focus on issues of mutual concern and growth of the class as a community. At these gatherings, children gain practice in listening to one another's perspectives and voicing their concerns while under the safe watch of the teacher.

SAFEGUARDING LEADERSHIP

If we truly wish to establish forums for children to develop a moral compass from which they can operate out on the playground—or out in the world— we need to broaden and deepen the expertise they already have in this richly educative subject of their school day—recess. The deep connection that children have with their teacher as being a symbol and provider of their safety and security cannot be underestimated. Mindful of that fundamental identity, we need to raise conversations about safety—the morals and ethics of compassionate behavior—to the forefront of a school's agenda.

In all of these conversations about behavior, rules, and moral development, the principal's job is to keep the child at the center of the school's purpose. The safeguarding dimension of leadership calls upon the principal to establish ongoing forums for faculty, for students, and for parents to explore issues related to students' physical and emotional well-being. A principal must support an atmosphere in which it is well accepted that the school's values are broader than subject matter competence, important as that may be. In fulfilling the safeguarding dimension of leadership, a school's principal must not only act fairly, thoughtfully, and justly, but be seen as someone who is proactive in the expectation that others will do so as well.

Knowing how students think, how they behave, how they react to disappointment, and how they demonstrate leadership and/or the skills needed to be a good team member will be enormously helpful information to guide them in their developing sense of ethics. It will also help the principal when it comes to that all-important task of organizing class groupings for the next school year, the subject matter of the following chapter.

LEADERSHIP LESSONS

- A school's principal can have a powerful effect on the development of children's moral behavior.
- A principal is obligated to serve as a wise moral leader in the eyes of the children (for teachers and parents as well) and that expected role requires imagination, empathy, and deeply grounded developmental insight. Being in the know about your students' behaviors, their growing but often faulty sense of what is acceptable and what is not, allows your interventions, when needed, to be more than keeper of the rules.
- For day-to-day transgressions, principals create their own continuum of disciplinary actions with intermediate steps that usually include reminders to the child(ren) to not do that again, or sitting out time for a child, or having the child write a letter of apology, or a letter to his/her parents to explain what happened.
- A good conversation with children exploring what's going on in their lives often serves to guide principals in choosing appropriate consequences.
- Principals and teachers are apt to overfocus on the particulars of the penalty, and lose sight of the overarching purpose of the disciplinary act, which is to reintegrate the wrongdoers into the community of students.
- Children are genuinely interested in knowing what's going on in other parts of the school. They are particularly interested in asking for the rationale behind certain rules and hearing about problems that occur when those rules are not followed. Access to these conversations helps young children gauge how safe they feel and how much they must know about the rules of the school.
- Principals can't settle for rules and regulations as the sole basis for their relationship with students under the assumption that a codified morality will have an impact on a child's development that is anything more than superficial.
- Principals have to assume the role of social anthropologist. You need to know how children of different ages think—what their normal behavior looks like and how they are likely to react to ethically com-

plex situations. New principals, especially, need to listen to the language of children that signals their level of conceptual understanding.

- In the classroom, teachers are the experts, but on the playground the kids are the experts. Kids know the curriculum of the playground, and we need to learn it from them. In order to balance the competing values, children and teachers need recess expectations embedded in the curriculum of the classroom, that place where safety can be assured.

Clarifying Episode:
A Parent Letter to the Principal

It was spring. We were well into our annual process of planning students' placement for the next school year. I was still new to the principalship and still learning how the parents were accustomed to communicating with their child's principal.

One late afternoon in my second year, I returned to my office after a meeting and found a single 3" x 5" card on my desk. Papers I had been working on were pushed aside so that the card could be clearly seen. It contained a child's name and a teacher's name—nothing more. I looked around my office quickly to be sure the card's messenger was not lurking in the corner or behind the door. Confirming I was alone, I considered some possible responses to this parent's "request": I could throw it out, I could put it in an unmarked envelope and mail it back to the family— postage due!, or I could take a deep breath and consider this 3" x 5" card as a sure signal that I needed to put a new process in place. After some further consideration of the "warts" with the current placement process, I chose option number three. I had no idea then how complex that task would turn out to be.

7

"Who'd You Get?": The Yearly Ritual of Classroom Placement

How did you find out who your teacher would be for next year and which kids would be in your class? Did her name appear at the bottom of your report card in June? Was there a list posted in the school's office over the summer? Did you wonder why you were put in that particular class? Whatever the process or method of notification, one thing is for sure: who you were going to get made a big difference in your life. Placing children into a particular classroom with a particular teacher still affects children enormously. As a principal your placement decisions will be a major factor in children's and their parents' opinion of and trust in you.

IN LATE August you hear a resounding buzz in the town—"Who'd you get?" The question is asked even more by parents than by children. The "who" is next year's teacher. Children and parents anxiously await the notification that sets off a chain of phone calls and grocery store conversations to compare their results. "Did we get the teacher we wanted?" "Did we get the *new* teacher?" "Which kids are in that class?" "I've heard she's nice." "Are any of his friends in that class?" "Oh, no! I've heard she's mean." All of these questions and sentiments point to two essential ingredients of a successful placement—a good teacher and the presence of friends.

PLACING STUDENTS: A HIGHLY VISIBLE FUNCTION
OF THE PRINCIPAL'S JOB

College courses could (and probably should) be offered on this single topic—placing children in class groupings for the coming year. It ranks as one of the most visible functions of the school principal. Having good teachers and knowing which kids are friends are excellent bases for this yearly ritual, but certainly not all that is needed to accomplish the job successfully. In fact, the student placement process consolidates many of the principal's leadership and management functions. Consider the skills needed to place children into class groupings for the coming year: planning and coordinating with staff; assessing the learning and social/emotional needs of each student; assessing each classroom teacher's strengths, weaknesses, teaching style, and interpersonal dispositions; addressing special education needs; assessing parental desires, if not demands; anticipating how each child's placement fits into a balanced grouping for learning; and educating parents and teachers about the process, to name just a few.

Balancing the subtle intermix of children's needs and wishes, teachers' dispositions, and parents' expectations requires considerable equilibrium, yet another opportunity for walking that tightrope. The most important resources for achieving that balance are "knowing" and "anticipating": knowing the children, knowing the teachers, knowing the parents, and, based on that knowing, anticipating how a placement will best serve the needs of each child. In the end, of course, that's what matters most.

"WE'VE ALWAYS DONE IT THIS WAY"

As a beginning principal I followed what I understood to be the chief mandate of an ill-defined class placement process: rely exclusively on the current classroom teachers for their recommendations. That seemed simple—at first; simple because I had no idea of the many layers of politics, psychological and emotional undercurrents, interpersonal complexities, and need for professional integrity that were embedded in this process. I did not yet possess that much-needed knowing about all the stakeholders.

The main transaction appeared to me to be between the classroom teacher and the parents. At that time I didn't realize how powerfully many parents influenced many teachers' decisions about a child's subsequent placement. Nor did teachers fully realize the extent to which they absorbed those parents' wishes into their own recommendation for a child's placement. To add to the complexity, I quickly learned that parents' and teachers' perceptions of each other's roles were contradictory. Many parents relied on their long-term relationship with a classroom teacher to get the placement matter taken care of as they wished, and they attributed final decision-making power to that teacher. Many teachers, however, were of the understanding that any parent could easily overturn a teacher's recommendation with a letter to the principal, who would be sure to acquiesce. Both parties were attributing placement power to each other, and so far, nobody was talking about my professional role and my placement power as the principal.

PARENT LETTERS

I had some idea that a child's placement was important to parents, but I was completely naïve about the political mechanisms underlying the process. A few parents made appointments to insure a preferred placement for their child. Many wrote an end-of-year letter to me telling me far more than I would have liked to know about their family (or sometimes another family in the community). If a family's older child had been placed with a particular teacher years ago, these parents spared no paper in telling me why they must or must not have that teacher for their younger child. They were well versed in the rumors about certain teachers. "She yells" or "she doesn't give homework" or "she doesn't like boys" or "it's past the time for her to retire!". Parents made explicit demands that their child be placed or not be placed with specific children. Other parents (actually, very few) considered letter-writing to be a disrespectful challenge to a principal's professional prerogative to assign children to classrooms. These few parents did nothing except to hope that the process worked and that (with luck!) their child would be with a good teacher next year.

I carefully studied that entrenched process for the first years to discover which parts were problematic and why. I was particularly interested in understanding the teachers' and parents' mind-sets about student placement and how their mind-sets shaped their roles in the process. What mattered to them? What were their priorities? What did they know about the teaching staff that I didn't know, and what would be an appropriate vehicle for me to receive this highly valuable information? And, of particular interest, what was my role to be?

SHHHHH! PLACEMENT POLITICS AT WORK

My study of the placement process revealed that there was a rampant sense in the community that political muscle was the major determinant of a child's placement. Some parents were perceived as powerful by other parents and skillful in getting their way. These powerful parents hoped to be perceived in just that way by the new principal as well. Rumors of meetings with me, initiated by powerful parents, spread through the parent community. "Well, I just went in there and told her who my child's teacher would be next year" was the gist of the reported interaction. Did I say interaction? I had no memory of these particular meetings having actually taken place. However, the feeling tone these rumors were intended to portray, both to the parents and to me, became apparent to me as they hoped it would. "My, my, my," I reflected. "How interesting." It was time to roll up my sleeves and put together a new plan.

I had finally discovered my role as perceived by parents and teachers. As principal, I was a necessary intermediary whose power would be derived from my ability to manage the placement process and to keep the many secrets held by each group. Principals are the sole recipients of all sorts of disclosures intended to influence the placement process (as with everything else in the school) in ways that support the wishes and hopes of individual stakeholders. A teacher may privately ask a principal to "Please don't put So-and-so's child in my class. I know they've asked for me and I've told them I really want to have Bobby in my class—but truly I don't." Or parents may confidentially amend a conversation with their child's current teacher in the form of a request to the principal: "I know we've had all of our children in Mrs. So-and-so's class but it really won't work for Billy. Of course we've told her that we're insisting that he be with her. We do love her." Or a teacher may reveal a hushed-voice sentiment to a principal that would be awkward for her to share with her teacher colleague: "Listen, I've told Gail that I really want Jenny in her classroom. Actually, I think Jenny would be lost in her room, but Gail and I are friends and I know she'd like Jenny in her class."

Principals must navigate all this often conflicting, self-serving, politically manipulated, and emotionally charged information; do the best possible thing for each child; and somehow keep all the parties involved reasonably happy. Beyond managing all that conflicting information, however, I needed to establish my leadership in this process by encouraging teachers and parents to become more confident that I, as the principal, am in the best position to balance all the factors entailed in this very complex process. Above all, their confidence in my role must accrue from the conviction that the principal is serving a single determining criterion for every placement, and that criterion is the best placement for each child's welfare.

EXAMINING THE PLACEMENT PROCESS: THE BASICS

The basics of the process that schools use to determine a child's class placement are remarkably similar across elementary schools everywhere. You have *x* number of students to divide into *x* number of classes. Enrollment, district guidelines, and budget will determine maximum class sizes. The rationale for grouping students will be guided by a school's philosophy and goals. Schools may group children by ability level, or mix ability levels into heterogeneous classes, or choose some combination of both kinds of groupings. So far, these steps could all be completed by a computer.

Now comes the human factor, the voices of the stakeholders who contribute varying amounts of information, hope, judgment, power, and perspective to the process. Students, teachers, parents, and principal have distinctive roles and mind-sets that need to be well choreographed into a process to best serve the interests and needs of each child when it comes to classroom placement.

MEET THE STAKEHOLDERS

Who are the stakeholders in deciding a child's classroom placement, and what useful knowledge do they bring to the process? The students' current classroom teachers logically play a major role in determining placement, although the power of the final decision is often reserved for the principal, who assumes responsibility for the placements. Next year's classroom teachers, that is, the receiving classroom teachers, as well as special subjects teachers (music, art, physical education, etc.) and special education teachers, can provide useful input into the process as well. The role of the parents will vary from school to school. The range of parent input spans from no parent input is allowed to straight-out parent requests for specific teachers. More often it is something in between. The last constituency, and certainly most important, are the students—the most interested stakeholders.

STUDENT THOUGHTS ABOUT PLACEMENT

Recently a 2nd-grader turned around to me in a student council meeting and asked, "Dr. Hebert, are you the one who tells kids what teachers they have?" I responded, "Yes." "Then could you put me in Mrs. Manley's class next year? She's nice. Oh, and put Devin Simon in that class, too—okay?" The child's mind-set on this topic is so clear and unambiguous—they want friends and a nice teacher.

Children are the most important stakeholders in the placement process and, ironically, the least vocal about their wishes and most resilient in adjusting their expectations. Their thoughts about placement are usually expressed to teachers and their parents. As spring approaches, classroom teachers glean useful information from their current students through various kinds of sociograms and/or interviews. Asking children, "Who's a good learning buddy? A good tablemate? Who's a good recess buddy?" yields good information that will assist teachers in organizing next year's class groupings. In addition, children tell their parents which kids they like and who's bothering them, and about a teacher they've seen in the hallway and who they have surmised is "nice." Parent letters to the principal often include these children's feelings and can be a rich source of information on behalf of the child.

PARENT THOUGHTS ABOUT PLACEMENT

The parents' concerns for their child's classroom placement are crystal clear. They want the best teacher for their child. In addition, they want their child with friends and away from bullies. Although they may not say so directly, the large majority of parents are pleased with their child's placement and teacher. Those parents who are not pleased, however, tend to let the principal know right away.

Fulfilling parents' wishes for their child's classroom placement is complicated by parents' understandable sole focus on their own child. Layers of additional complexity in the parents' perspective may include unpleasant memories of their own elementary years, and a mistrust of authority in general and of schools in particular. The premise of this mistrust is that the schools are the "them" of an "us/them" culture. Following this thinking, assumptions are made: (1) The lineup of teachers for the following year carries a ranking along a continuum from good to not good, (2) there are powerful and less powerful parents, (3) the powerful ones get the teacher they request. It's likely that the parents of these parents wouldn't have dreamed of offering their opinion about their child's teacher for the coming year. One wonders where this absence of trust began and why. And more important, what can schools do to regain parent trust?

TEACHER THOUGHTS ABOUT PLACEMENT

The voice of the classroom teachers is crucial to the placement process. Teachers possess significant knowledge and perspective about their students that is invaluable in the process of placing students for the following school year. However, there are other teachers in the building who know these children well. So it's important for a principal to hear and differentiate the concerns of a classroom teacher from a special education teacher from a special subjects teacher—all contributors to a child's successful placement.

A Current Classroom Teacher's Mind-Set

Classroom teachers readily assume their role as the primary contributor of information in the placement process. They bring a deep knowledge of their students—their academic skills, behavior patterns, friendships, and parental expectations—to the placement discussion. A complicating factor, however, is that classroom teachers also bring an ambitious agenda of highly personalized goals, some of which are not able to be realized because they supersede the teacher's knowledge or conflict with other goals that must be taken into account beyond what teachers are likely to be aware of.

Among their many goals, classroom teachers feel strongly about not wanting to overburden next year's teacher—a colleague—with too many needful students and/or difficult parents. In aid of achieving that goal, the balance of each group is an important factor to monitor. Following that initial hope, classroom teachers wish to place each child with the "right teacher" who will do the best job with this child. At the same time, they want to place each child with at least one or two friends. In addition, most classroom teachers want to anticipate parental wishes for separating particular children from each other as well as facilitating hoped-for friendships.

With so many goals in mind, classroom teachers need a well-defined process to help them put their priorities in order, to share this important responsibility with colleagues and their principal, and to relieve them of the self-imposed burden of "doing it all." It's important for the principal to recognize that as thoroughly as classroom teachers know their own students, their knowledge of the other students at that same grade level is likely to be minimal. More important to note is that teachers' knowledge of their colleagues' teaching style is surprisingly limited (Barth, 1984, p. 24).

Next Year's Classroom Teacher's Mind-Set

Classroom teachers have dual mind-sets, depending on whether they are the sending teacher or the receiving teacher. Next year's classroom teacher longs to have a "good class," meaning a small number of well-behaved students who all want to learn. Additional characteristics of a good class include: children from families they've had a good relationship with, few new families with whom relationship and trust need to be established, a manageable range of heterogeneity in the academic span, and, worth repeating, no behavior problems!

It's customary for classroom teachers to peruse the list of all upcoming students to their grade level and to let the principal know of any families whose child would be best placed in another teacher's classroom. Good reasons for this request include a past unsuccessful relationship with a particular family's older child, or a personal/professional relationship with a family that would create some complications. "My husband works in the same office as this dad," or "we have a social relationship with this couple," or "that mom is my gynecologist," or "I've already had to work with that family, thank you" are comments that a principal may hear from next year's teacher.

A Special Subjects Teacher's Mind-Set

An often overlooked voice in the placement process is that of the special subjects teachers (music, art, physical education, library). These teachers have taught different permutations of each grouping over the years and have good insights into what has and what hasn't worked. Practically speaking, teachers who have long-term experience and knowledge of children over consecutive years offer uniquely valuable information that contributes a much-needed perspective to the large placement puzzle. The special subjects teachers know all the children; their participation serves to balance out those knowledge holes that classroom teachers can't fill.

Special subjects teachers are accustomed to working with large groups, so they have a unique expertise in assessing the dynamics of each classroom grouping. A physical education teacher can quickly scan a class list and assess the balance of leadership and good sportsmanship. A music or art teacher notes a group's cohesiveness as they scan these same class lists. These teachers are good at spotting creative children who would benefit from having a similar kind of child in their classroom.

Unlike the classroom teachers, who are organizing this group of children to send on to their colleagues at the next grade level, the special subjects teachers are usually both the sender and the receiver of the group. In general, special subjects teachers know all the students and which groups work well or don't work well together.

A Special Education Teacher's Mind-Set

Special education teachers know fewer students; however, they know these few children and their parents extremely well. Their goal is to have those students on their caseloads with classroom teachers whose style most closely replicates what special education children require to support their learning deficits and goals. In looking at class groupings, special education teachers are seeking those classroom teacher colleagues whose style includes clarity, organization, willingness to adjust or extend their assignments, and the ability to team with another educator in supporting a particular child's specialized needs. Special education teachers are particularly seeking a good collegial relationship that results in good collaborative planning.

In addition, scheduling is on their minds. Special education teachers like to cluster children in classrooms to facilitate their schedules. Having more than one child of similar needs in a classroom allows them to work more efficiently and is, therefore, desirable for them.

Special education teachers have an additional unique responsibility in the school. These educators develop long-term collaborative relationships with particular classroom teachers. As teachers move to another grade level or retire and new teachers are hired, the special education teachers have the unassigned but required responsibility to educate their new colleagues about the dynamics of the collaborative relationship between special education and the classroom so that children's needs can be addressed. Their advocacy for a child's placement with a particular teacher may at times appear burdensome to the placement process, but it needs to be considered in light of their responsibilities to educate new colleagues and their insightful perspectives.

TEACHER CULTURE: A DEEPER LOOK

Beyond the mind-set of each stakeholder group is the even more complex issue of teacher–mindset interactions, which often ricochet off each other in subtle and puzzling ways. Knowing how teachers' differing perspectives affect the dynamics of the student placement process is crucial for the principal, who needs to keep all of this thinking and flow of information in productive balance as the placement process unfolds.

One reason for this complex interplay of teachers' perspectives is that teachers seldom see each other teach. It's reasonable for a principal to assume that teachers who know one another well also know the realities of each other's teaching, and, of specific relevance to placing students in classrooms, how the particulars of a colleague's classroom environment might be experienced by children. It may sound counterintuitive to disagree with this assumption, but it's simply not the case. There's good reason for that. Teachers have little time, if any, to be in one another's classrooms and, of more significance, they have a certain ambivalence about their wish to get to know one another's work as teachers.

Professional Autonomy versus Professional Growth: Competing Values

Despite encouraging teachers to visit one another's classrooms, many teachers feel uncomfortable observing each other or being observed. One of Roland Barth's (1984) well-known insightful images alludes to issues of authentic collegiality at all levels of schooling. In this description, Barth beautifully captures a well-known persistent tension in schools: professional autonomy versus professional growth.

> Teachers and administrators develop subtle ways to influence the other group's domain, but they seldom venture there. A 3rd grade teacher on one side of the hall carefully respects the teaching space of the 3rd grade teacher on the other side. One principal in a system seldom visits the school of another. . . . We all seem to have an implied contract: Don't bother me in my work and I won't bother you. Yet in schools, as in sandboxes, the price of doing things the way we want to—of having personal control over what we do—is isolation from others who might take our time and have us do things differently (and, perhaps, better). (p. 24)

It would seem logical that teachers would want to take full advantage of any opportunity to observe another teacher as a way to assist with the goal of refining their own instructional skills. Ironically, most teachers do not see it that way. Their wish for professional autonomy and individualism exceeds their ability, and even their wish, to take a good look at their own teaching and to be open to the possibilities that self-reflection may entail, perhaps having to teach in a different way.

Teachers often substitute friendship for professional collegiality and are successful in engendering fellowships with that goal in mind. Their social bonds and spirit of community are a precious commodity, so they do not want to be privy to information gleaned through direct observation that may intrude on their personal relationships with one another. There is an unstated fear that professional observation will reveal inadequacies not perceivable beyond the level of close friendship or administrative evaluation. Teachers spend endless hours talking *about* their teaching, *about* their students, *about* what works and what hasn't worked in their classrooms. One would assume that with all of this conversation about their classrooms, teachers would know the realities of one another's teaching quite well. The truth is that talking about teaching and witnessing actual teaching are two entirely different phenomena. The extent to which teachers' actual practice contradicts their self-perception is the business of principals—a business that teachers do not want any part of, as applied either to themselves or to their colleagues.

"Linda's So Good With That Kind of Kid"

Still, teachers maintain strong, nevertheless often ungrounded, opinions about their colleagues' teaching abilities. "Linda's so good with those special needs students," or "Bob doesn't really challenge those high-achieving kids," or "Jenny'd be lost in Gail's class." How do teachers form these opinions if they don't have time to be in one another's classrooms? One way is that teachers often hear the opinions of parents or special education teachers and staff who may have a more legitimate presence in those classrooms, not fully realizing that these assessments may be focused on that teacher's relationship with a particular few children. During parent–teacher conferences, clouded in words of admiration and hoping to shape the upcoming experience, a parent is apt to voice their child's report of the prior year's teacher's capabilities: "Steven was so confused in 3rd grade; he liked Mrs. Randall but every day he'd come home and wonder why the kids were so noisy and why she couldn't control the class. Dave and I are so happy he's with you this year."

Still another rationale for this unqualified opinion syndrome is that, absent any of these inputs, people simply form opinions. It seems that we can't help but formulate some judgment of a colleague. If asked, we don't really know the source of that subconscious assumption—we just think of them that way.

Warning! This Child/Family Is Not Easy

The opinions we hold of our colleagues often form the basis for a classroom teacher's wish for a child to be in a particular classroom. "This kid is difficult; he needs to be with Karen." Maybe; maybe not. What does this teacher actually know about Karen's classroom that supports that recommendation? Unsupported opinions and/or limited knowledge of a colleague's teaching tends to impede a primary goal of the classroom teacher—not to burden their colleague with too many difficult children or parents.

Teachers don't fully realize that what's difficult for them may not be difficult for their colleague. Teachers possess differing capacities and varying levels of tolerance for certain kinds of children and their parents. An observant principal will watch carefully to see what kinds of children thrive with particular teachers and, conversely, which children and families "push the wrong buttons" for each teacher. Over time, principals are obligated to glean this kind of knowledge unavailable to anyone else, and to act on that knowledge to the best interests of both students and teachers.

Teacher–Parent Interactions: Uncomfortable Hallway Conversations

The parent perception of the classroom teacher's power in the placement process leads to frequent hallway conferences in the spring, when parents start petitioning for the "best teacher" for their child for the following year. Teachers are uncomfortable with these conversations that invite them to voice opinions about their colleagues and possibly to enter into some secret agreement with a parent. They know all too well that they also are apt to be the subject of such a conversation as they glance down the hall to see a colleague and a parent in a hushed interaction.

Another problem with these sidebar conversations is that lots of people engage in promise-making. How can all these promises be kept? Teachers need to be protected from this "open season placement frenzy" and to be provided with language to use to respond to parents when asked about placement. The tone of their response is important. Language is needed that would effectively move the issue off their plate and onto mine. "Sounds like you have some concerns. Have you written your letter to the principal? She needs to know about your concerns," or "I'm certainly part of the process, but I don't make the final decisions," are some good phrases for teachers to have in their back pocket.

PRINCIPAL THOUGHTS ABOUT PLACEMENT

A principal's greatest wish is that the parent community trust the school (and its principal!) and that the errors in judgment we make from time to time can, with good will, be resolved out of that trustful relationship. Pertaining specifically to placement, a principal's uncomplicated hope is to have happy children taught by happy teachers resulting in happy parents.

As principal, you have the central responsibility (and unenviable job) of trying to make sense of all the stakeholders' mind-sets, suggestions, and demands and then to finalize a plan for student placements that will be considerate of all you know and all they know as well. A principal needs to "stay on the dance floor" to gather and understand the variety of mind-sets of all of the other stakeholders. Then the principal needs to move to the balcony to balance all of their wishes, inject his/her own knowledge, and consolidate this information, all the while staying focused on the needs of individual children.

The challenge is how to organize and consolidate all of that information so that it can be usefully accessed when it's needed. Principals utilize a wide variety of techniques for getting to know and remembering information and impressions about the students. Many use a picture Rolodex with student names just to have a quick reminder of a child's name & face. In addition, many maintain a log of some kind that helps them capture memorable moments about a child (such as reading with a child in a first-grade classroom), or a conversation with a parent about a concern, or a disciplinary incident with a student.

A PROCESS FOR PLACING STUDENTS: THE SPECIFICS

Principals know their faculty well and will get to know most of the parents. As we sort and sift through all of this relevant and important information, we make full use of that knowledge to calibrate all of the inputs. At some point in the spring and well into the summer, you will begin tackling what is essentially your responsibility and prerogative—guiding the placement process, involving all the stakeholders as appropriate, and making the final decisions about each child's placement for the upcoming school year.

Over a period of many years, a process has been developed at our school that I believe works well in considering all the variables and details that need to be attended to in placing children.

March: Letter to Parents

It begins with a letter (similar to the one shown in figure 7.1) to all parents that invites them to share their thoughts about their child's progress and concerns for next year. In order to democratize the process, it made sense to me to solicit letters from all parents so that everyone would have an opportunity, if not an obligation, to let me know their thoughts about their child's placement for the coming year. Each year the letter is mailed the week prior to spring break.

A parent response form accompanies the letter and asks two questions: "How did this year go for your child?" and "What do you want me to think about in placing your child for next year?" Getting feedback about the current year helps me to decode parents' thoughts about the school and their goals for their child. Parents are specifically asked not to request a particular teacher. On a practical level, if a parent requests a particular teacher who does not return the following year, or changes grade levels, that parent's letter gives me little useful information about a parent's concerns for their child. Also, a parent's request for a particular teacher is often based on what they've heard from another parent, which may or may not be relevant to the needs of their child. Newer teachers are less known by the parent community, and so their names may not be "out there" as much as the names of more senior teachers. For all such reasons, it is best to openly discourage requests for specific teachers.

On the Reflection Form parents are also asked whether they'd like this letter to be shared with next year's teacher, or if it is intended "For Principal's Eyes Only." This question was added only a few years ago and has clarified the audience for the parent letter. Finally, a due date of early May is given (good luck with that!). Once letters are received, they are set aside to be read

FIGURE 7.1. Letters to Parents—Student Placement

March 2005

Dear Parents,

During the next few weeks, the teachers and I will be meeting to begin planning your child's placement for the 2005–2006 school year. Each student's placement will be carefully considered in light of all areas of development, including intellectual, social, and emotional.

Each year I ask parents to share with me, in writing, their thoughts regarding their child. Again this year I am adding a bit more structure to this request, as I find that my yearly letter to you is often misread as "a teacher request letter." I am attaching a form to this letter, and I ask that you not indicate a preference for a particular teacher.

Please return this form to my office no later than **Friday, May 6**. Parents of first–fourth graders will be notified of teacher placement in late August at which time we will be back in the office.

I will be talking about the process of student placement at an evening meeting on **Thursday, April 14, at 7:00**. Please join me that evening so that I can address questions you may have. I appreciate the time you take to complete this form as your thoughts are helpful to me in planning student groupings for next year.

Sincerely,

Elizabeth A. Hebert
Principal

Child's Current Grade Level _____

REFLECTIONS ON THE CURRENT YEAR
& THINKING AHEAD TO NEXT YEAR
FOR

_____
Child's Name

How do you think your child's current school year is progressing so far?

Indicate below any other information you would like me to consider in placing him/her for the coming school year. Do not indicate any preference for a specific teacher.

Complete one form for each child who will be attending Crow Island (grades 1–4 for 2005–2006). Please return this form to my office no later than Friday, **May 6, 2005.**

_____ Please share this letter with next year's teacher.
_____ Do not share this letter. For Principal only.

at a later time, the reason for which I explain to parents at a subsequent evening meeting. I tell parents that "I need to be guided by your letters and protected from your letters as well. Due to some specific requests for placing your child with another child, or separating your child from another child, I need to have a good draft in place, before I read your letter, that represents our best knowledge of all the many dynamics and to consider your requests in light of those discussions with teachers."

March: Packets to Teachers

In that same week prior to spring break, classroom teachers will find a placement packet in their mailboxes. It contains individual pictures of their current students from the office Rolodex, along with a listing of each student and their history of placement, that is, which teachers each child had for prior grade levels. (See figure 7.2 for a sample placement grid.)

This listing provides useful data for both teacher and principal. Aided by the grid, the teacher can be reminded of which children each child has been in class with in prior years. From a principal's perspective, the placement history provides trend information at a glance that influences placement decisions. Has a child been placed with several first-year or new teachers or more than one teacher who has left for maternity leave? Such a placement profile will be perceived by parents as less positive than that of a child who has been placed with more experienced teachers in consecutive years uninterrupted by a leave of absence. Equity on this issue is always a goal, but is only one of a myriad of complex factors that must be considered.

A memo accompanies the packet asking the teachers to schedule a time to meet with me in grade-level teams to complete a preliminary first draft of student groupings. The teachers are asked to select a two-hour block of time (substitute coverage will be provided) when we can come together to put together a good first draft of groupings for next year. A representative from the special subjects teachers (music, art, PE, library) and the Pupil Services Team (special education) also attend these planning meetings. This enhancement to the placement process has been critical both practically and symbolically. Practically, as has been mentioned, these special subjects teachers know all the students over time—a much-needed perspective in these discussions. Symbolically, the presence of the special subjects and special education teachers is a much-needed reminder to classroom teachers that these colleagues share in the instructional program for each child and that their invaluable insights need to be considered in the placement conversation.

FIGURE 7.2. History of Student Placement Grid

Placement History: Ms. Yoshida, 3rd-Grade Class

First Name	Birthdate	Teacher		
		2nd Grade	1st Grade	Kindergarten
Bennett	6/19/96	Hart	Simon	Gira
Roger	9/15/95	Davis	Simon	Karaganis
Aidan	9/15/96	Hoferle	Kilb	Karaganis
Will	12/4/95	Davis	Manley	Gira
Louis	3/31/96	Reimer	Simon	Gira
Edward	10/14/95	Hoferle	Simon	Gira
Michael	4/8/96	Hart	Manley	Saunders
Bernard	12/27/95	Hart	Kilb	Saunders
Richard	9/7/95	Davis	Kilb	Karaganis
Paul	4/8/96	Reimer	Hummel	Saunders
Ann	12/16/95	Reimer	Simon	Gira
Erica	3/12/96	Stoioff	Manley	Saunders
Kathleen	8/1/96	Hart	Hummel	Gira
Jan	9/29/95	Stoioff	Manley	Karaganis
Becky	12/1/95	Stoioff	Kilb	Saunders
Terry	10/25/95	Reimer	Kilb	Gira
Martha	9/25/95	Hart	Kilb	Gira
Catherine	9/25/95	Hoferle	Simon	Gira
Valerie	3/6/96	Davis	Hummel	Karaganis
Laura	5/14/96	Davis	Hummel	Saunders
Olivia	6/15/96	Reimer	Simon	Saunders

April: Parent Meeting About the Placement Process

The March letter invites parents to an evening meeting at which I review and clarify the placement process to them. I begin by having the parents think back to their own childhoods and try to remember how they found out who their teacher for the coming year would be. I reflect on the fact that the process has become far more complex than when they were in school. Our school's goal is to create student groupings that are heterogeneous—balanced for academics and leadership. I explain the process we have in place in some detail, but more important, I emphasize the extensive thought that goes into each child's placement. I describe the series of meetings with the classroom teachers as well as special subjects teachers and special education teachers. I encourage them to write letters, and I explain how their letters will be used in the later stages of the process.

April/May: Meetings with Teachers

Each grade-level group of teachers, a special subjects teacher, a special education teacher, and I gather at the agreed-upon time in a room with a chalkboard. There are four columns (or as many class sections as needed for that grade level) on the chalkboard labeled "Group A," "Group B," "Group C," and "Group D." These letters will be replaced in a later draft with the names of teachers for that grade level. I have the distinctive obligation and honor (!) of matching teacher names to each grouping. We've learned over the years that starting with teacher names clouds the process because sending teachers tend to be overly influenced by their own perceptions of their receiving teacher colleagues.

I review the process for any new teacher on the team. Our goal is to put together a good first draft of balanced, heterogeneous groups of students. In planning these groupings, we'll focus on students' learning needs, behavior, leadership, and social needs. Which children learn and/or play well together? Which children learn/play better when separated in different classrooms?

Another way for us to define "balance" is that all of the receiving teachers (yet to be assigned one of these groups) should be able to look at one another's class lists and perceive their groups as equal in strengths and needs. We must be careful in constructing each group so that one or two classrooms are not clearly more onerous than the others. These are all very complex goals to achieve. We proceed slowly.

We begin with "anchor children" or "leadership clusters." "Anchor children" is our code for students whose learning needs are extensive or whose behavioral regulation will probably require more time from the teacher than other students in the classroom. An anchor student could also be a child who does not demonstrate any unusual learning needs, but whose parents have communication needs that are extensive and will require more than usual attention by the teacher.

"Leadership clusters" refer to one or more students who provide balanced leadership in a group. A leader may be a child of any academic skill level. Their leadership quality is defined by strong interpersonal skills and positive dispositions that have been consistently demonstrated. These children have come to be known as leaders in that sense.

Over the next 2 hours each teacher will suggest student groupings that I will record under each of the A, B, C, and D columns until we all feel we have the beginnings of that much-desired balance in each group. As we tentatively assign a child to each group, the teachers explain their placement judgment with a brief description that helps inform the entire group about this child's needs. ("Johnny's a great student—tops in all subjects, but he's fiercely competitive and that has an impact on the group." Or, "Claire has lots of learning needs but adds a positive leadership strength to the group.") Throughout this process, I am eyeing the board and sifting the names of next year's teachers in my mind. At the same time, the special education staff and/ or the special subjects teachers are offering their long-term thinking as the groups are shaped. Throughout the process, we stop often, take a look at where we are, and check out how we're feeling about the balance in the accumulating groups.

The Winnetka Public Schools' philosophy (1981) is committed to the benefits of heterogeneous groupings of students. However, the "bandwidth" of heterogeneity within any classroom is an important consideration in achieving those intended benefits. Most classroom teachers find that a classroom group comprised of a cluster of academically talented students and a cluster of students with extensive academic needs, but with few or no students in the midrange, is the most difficult group to have because it approximates teaching two grade levels simultaneously. We attempt to cluster students of similar needs in each classroom and keep an eye on a workable range of heterogeneity.

Group Rankings

At the end of this 2-hour meeting, I ask the teachers to rank the groupings we've just created. "Take a look at these four groupings. Pretend you're the receiving teacher of one of these groups. Based on what you know about each group, jot down your first, second, third, and last-choice grouping of students." The goal of this activity is to check to see if we have, in fact, reasonably balanced groupings. If all of the teachers at this meeting have different preferences for their number-one choice—that's good. If, on the other hand, all of the teachers at this meeting rank Group C as their first choice and Group A as their least favorite, that's a strong indication that we need to reassign students from Group C over to Group A in order to redress the imbalances that have crept in.

Although this initial meeting serves as a good focused beginning conversation, we go through 2 to sometimes more than 10 drafts of these lists from April to August. We rarely, if ever, complete a final draft at the initial meeting.

These student placement conversations achieve other important goals for enhancing faculty cohesiveness. We organize our placement process around guidelines: our loose set of rules that defines for us what a good class grouping consists of. The guidelines, however, focus our attention on articulating the overarching rationale for placing children together or separately. And it's the talking about each child—not the guidelines—that is the crucial achievement of the placement process. Taking time to say why on behalf of each child is time-consuming and difficult. But once it's done, you've achieved classroom groupings that are well planned and thoughtfully designed. Taking the time to anticipate each child's comfort for the coming year is good for the child and good for us. Sharing our thoughts/vulnerabilities/ideas about each child lets us know one another as professionals in a way that no other conversation can accomplish.

Reflections on a Class List—Pulling It All Together

I look at one of the proposed class lists. Now is the time to make use of that all-important knowing that only a principal possesses. With experience I have come to be able to see students' faces without the aid of a Rolodex. I know these children well. I watch them play, I watch them read, I interact with them in the many different scenes of the school day. I know this particular child learns quickly and makes friends easily. I know this other child on this same class list struggles academically and socially as well. Oh, and here's my "energetic friend"—a terrific kid, but eats up his share of a teacher's time, and then some. If we can just get him through his final elementary grades.

I also know the parents. Hallway conversations and phone calls flash in my mind. A family's history with this teacher—has it been positive? This other student's mother has a tendency to overwhelm a newer teacher. A confidential conversation with a parent about a failing friendship or a fear of a particular child's influence on their son. A helpful and supportive parent. A tough parent. A worried parent.

And, of course, I know the teachers. I consider their many strengths, their vulnerabilities, what sets them off balance, what kind of child thrives in their presence. Although I've done everything I can to put together a grade-level team of teachers who are all equally ideal, that is a goal never perfectly achieved—at least in the parents' eyes. Beyond parents' wishes, though, I've worked to put together grade-level teams of teachers in which each one is different enough to accommodate different needs of the students and, at the same time, similar enough to work together and share ideas.

Since I am part of the placement discussions with the teachers, the balance of the groupings has already been considered extensively. Now, finally, I face the need to replace the "A," "B," "C," and "D," headings with four classroom teacher names. I make an initial assignment—Teacher X with Group A. How does that look to me? Hmmmm, good, except for these two children. One child's brother was in her classroom and the family had concerns. I don't think this child's needs will be best served in that placement. Another child in this same class had a bullying relationship with a boy now assigned to this group—we missed that in the grouping discussions. I look to the other groups to replace this boy. I shift a few more students, but not too many. Then I assign Group B to a teacher and repeat the examination for good fit. And so on for the rest.

I confer with the current teachers about my decisions. Now, with teacher names on the lists, the teachers make a few more suggestions for changes. I agree sometimes; sometimes not. Finally, after trying each teacher with each grouping and completing some fine-tuning, I feel I've made the best possible assignments. I set the lists aside for some time to let it all settle and then I look again. Yes, these groups seem to work. Now, the parent letters.

May: Review Parent Letters

Once I feel we have a good almost-final draft of each class list, I turn to the parent letters that I've already received (but set aside) for further guidance and to check myself on how well we've anticipated their perspective about their child's placement for the coming year. In some cases, I'll note a parent's comment that makes me reconsider a particular placement seriously enough that I call that parent, discuss the placement, and ask if their wish for, say, a separation from a particular child as expressed in that letter to me is their primary focus for their child's placement. Parents are almost always grateful for this vigilance and concern and often reconsider their initial request.

June/July/August: Finalize Lists

The lists are set aside in anticipation of inevitable family moves during the summer and new families moving in. By the third week in August I've made the necessary adjustments and revisions and am ready for the "big bang"—notifying everyone of their child's class assignment for the upcoming year. I have continued the practice already in place when I became principal, of sending individual notifications, like the one in figure 7.3, to families, rather than a class list, in order to personalize each child's classroom placement.

August/September: Phone Calls/Meetings about Placement

Inevitably, some parents will not be pleased with their child's teacher assignment for the coming year. The process you set in place is only as good as

FIGURE 7.3. Sample Placement Postcard

CROW ISLAND SCHOOL
1112 Willow Rd.
Winnetka, Illinois 60093

Your child, _____, has been

assigned to _____'s

_____ grade classroom.

The opening day of school will be

Monday, August 29. (Dismissal at 11:25 a.m.)

Elizabeth A. Hebert
Principal

your teaching staff. If you have weak teachers or teachers who are rumored or known to be less enthusiastic or less competent than their peers, you will hear from parents who will request a change in placement. This is an issue that all principals face, and the parents' eyes (and teachers' eyes) are watching closely. Will you change a child's placement?

All principals cope with this request in ways they feel best serve the specifics of that situation as well as the process as a whole. There will always be instances where the concern a parent has is well grounded. In these instances a principal needs to simply acknowledge an error and rectify the situation by changing the child's placement. If you've made an error in judgment and honestly feel this child's needs would not be well served in that particular classroom, you should probably make that change. If, on the other hand, you honestly feel the placement is more than adequate, you should consider maintaining the child in that classroom despite parental petition to change it. Over the years, I've experienced some heated conversations, letters, and phone calls that urge me to consider changing a placement. Over time, most parents come to trust the process. It's important to note, however, that your placement process will be considered trustworthy only if your staffing decisions merit that trust.

REFLECTIONS ON THE PLACEMENT PROCESS

So we get back to the central goals of placing children—being with friends and a good teacher who cares about children. We take this responsibility seriously and in so doing, we may sometimes overestimate or underestimate a child's resilience as well as a teacher's competence. Try as we may, we simply are unable to perfectly predict the real interaction between "this child" and "this teacher," or between "this child" and "these other children." Still, it makes more than good sense to go through the process because, in fact, it is the process that is more important than its outcome. The process clearly makes the statement to all that despite any flaws, we must make these decisions in a way that is as reasonable and fair as possible and, most important, that signals the value of an unflagging concern for each child. Roland Barth (1980) states it well:

> Perhaps then, the real importance of the arduous annual placement process lies less in its particular outcome . . . than in the process itself. Placement provides an annual occasion for all members of the school community to demonstrate their commitment to children. It becomes a time when adults can work together intensely for children, forging bonds of trust, interdependence, confidence, respect and cooperation. (p. 93)

Placing students into classes for the coming year is a highly visible as well as politically and psychologically influential function of the principal's job. Assuming responsibility for knowing all the stakeholders, coordinating all of their concerns, and then anticipating how each placement will best serve the needs of each child is an enormous enterprise. Taking the responsibility for such important decisions is one of many instances when a principal's authority and leadership is displayed to the public eye. That authority and that leadership, as we shall see, carries with it the inevitable burden of administrative aloneness.

LEADERSHIP LESSONS

- Placing students into classrooms ranks as one of the most visible and sensitive functions of the school principal.
- The most complex issue of classroom placement is anticipating that subtle intermix of children's needs, teachers' dispositions, and parents' expectations.

- The stakeholders include students, teachers, parents, and principal. An important step for the principal is to understand each group's mind-set and expectations.
- A well-defined placement process, known to all, will be of great benefit to a principal as well as to the image of the school as a fair and humane environment.
- All principals need to confront the issue of whether they will change a placement upon receiving a request (or demand) from a parent.
- A thoughtful placement process makes the clear statement to all that despite any flaws we must make these decisions in a way that is as reasonable and fair as possible and, most important, that signals the value of an unflagging concern for each child.

Clarifying Episode:
A Principal's Lunch

A new 2nd grader is with us in the lunch program today. I watch him seated between the two boys assigned as his buddies, cautiously opening his lunch bag while eyeing the contents of his new friends' lunches. He is measuring the quality of his own midday meal against the expected norm. To his great relief, both he and his lunch pass with flying colors.

I remember my own first lunch at school—as principal. Nobody had assigned me a couple of lunchtime buddies, so I was pretty much on my own to sort out the many subtle, complex dimensions of this ritual. When would I have my lunch? And more stressful to think about, where would I eat it? If I ate in the faculty lounge, where would I sit?

I have a vivid memory of nervously striding (but trying to look casual) into the lounge on that first day with an apple and draping myself over the refrigerator. An apple didn't require a plate or silverware that would cause me to interfere with the crowd at the sink or in any way intrude on busy teachers' lunch routines carefully calibrated to ensure their prompt return to classrooms. It was also a strategic position that afforded me an opportunity to efficiently chat with everyone—they all went to the refrigerator.

Most important, I did not want to presume to take a seat at one of the tables—maybe that was someone's chair. Have you ever watched a substitute teacher come into the teacher's lounge and take a seat at one of the tables—a seat usually occupied by a particular teacher? It's hilarious! Everyone comes in as usual, notes the change in seating, and goes about their business, somewhat nervously waiting for their colleague to come in. How will she handle it? In some schools, I've actually witnessed teachers politely leaning over to a substitute and saying, "Excuse me, that's Helen's chair—you may want to sit over there," motioning to a less frequented area of the lounge with easy access to yesterday's newspaper. Once you've seen that, trust me, you'll never forget it, and you'll never want that said to you.

I attempted this ritual only a few more times. I soon recognized that shift in teacher conversation when I came into the lounge, that few decibels' change in loudness that signaled a certain discomfort. I was grateful to have meetings or playground duty as a reason not to be in the lounge at lunchtime. So I grabbed my apple or my yogurt and discreetly found other places to go.

8

Administrative Aloneness: The Darker Side of the Principalship

---

The principalship has not been what I originally imagined. It has been far more rewarding and fulfilling, certainly more energy-consuming, and considerably more complex than I envisioned. Having authority over others is a troublesome matter. As a principal, that authority has had to be exercised in my many decisions over the last two decades. Most were mundane; many were readily regarded as positive; but a few (and it only takes one) provoked reactions from others that caused me to experience intense feelings of aloneness. The unanticipated conflicts arising as a consequence of those particular decisions illuminated, for me, the inevitable reality that having authority demands, a separation from those you lead. This is a most perplexing reality of the leadership life.

VISITS TO kindergarten continue to be the best way to start my day. As I mentioned in Chapter 2 in recounting how this book got its title, "*The Boss of the Whole School*," five-year-olds generously share a practical perspective on life's complex matters that keeps principals coming back for more of their gems of wisdom. Kindergartners have a unique way of welcoming visitors. They note your presence with some initial caution while they graciously invite you to occupy a vacant chair at their snack table or include you as a character in a play just now being staged in the block corner. This is especially true in the beginning of the year when school is still new to them. That's how it happened on one of my recent visits to kindergarten. Except one more thing: on this particular visit, I discovered a secret about being a principal.

DISCOVERING THE SECRET

On that morning I was greeted with the usual hugs and invitations to join individual children in their many activities throughout the room. The teacher noted my presence and, as part of the routine reinforcement of who's-who-in-the-school, she happily announced a greeting to me in her teacher voice, "Boys and girls, look who's here. Do we know who this is?"

Before any group response could be composed, one confident boy shouted out, "Sure, she's the princess." And then very quietly, but just barely within my hearing, a follow-up remark to his playmate: "I don't think she's mean—do you?" The other boy didn't respond; he just pondered the question. Without indicating to them that I overheard this speculation, I, too, pondered the question. I was fascinated by the proposed connection: "principal = princess = mean?" I suppressed my impulse to ask the obvious question: "So, how come you think principals are mean?" I recognized that he was just then forming this hypothesis in his own mind.

The kindergarteners smiled and nodded at Jonathan's reference to me as the "princess." His confused substitution of "princess" for "principal," two words that not only sound alike but also share overlapping meanings, seemed to satisfy their concept of who I was. Young children are very tolerant of one another's confusions and errors because they understand how hard it is to answer all the many questions you are asked in school. A few children who knew I was called the "principal" did not correct their classmate; instead they called out to me by name to show their fellow students their precise knowledge of my identity. The teacher and I exchanged conspiratorial smiles. Certainly, neither of us would correct this child's delightful miscue. We added it to the long list of amusing kindergartenisms, a story surely to be retold at every opportunity to colleagues and parents.

Principals are accustomed to overhearing remarks or exchanges not intended for administrative ears. As I go about the "busyness" of my day, I sort the many conversations or observations, and I often recognize a remark or an interaction as significant enough for further reflection. Something about it signals noteworthiness and so I tuck it away in a mental file, confident that it will be dislodged at a later time, and given a context and a space to be examined. That's how it happened with Jonathan's comment.

ADMINISTRATIVE ALONENESS

Months later, I was cleaning out my briefcase (a once a year chore) and again came across "Lonely at the Top: Observations on the Genesis of Administrative Isolation" by Philip Jackson, a former director of the University of

Chicago Laboratory Schools and a distinguished educational writer and philosopher (Jackson, 1977). Twenty-one years ago, as a brand-new principal, I read Jackson's paper for the first time. My superintendent gave a copy to the principals in our small school district. I wasn't ready for Jackson's ideas about a gripping reality of the leadership life not yet imagined by me. Youth and naïveté were my natural defenses against what appeared to me to be Jackson's emphasis on the darker side of the principalship. I thought to myself, "Why would a principal feel lonely and isolated? I don't feel lonely; I'm happy. I like what I do, and I think people like me." Still, I recognized Jackson's deep feeling and riveting insights about the aloneness of a school's leader as something I should keep in mind, so I hung onto the article—quite literally. I kept it in my briefcase for many years and occasionally glanced at it to remind myself of its message.

Now, as a veteran principal, I realize that I've not only come to appreciate the veracity of Jackson's article, but find it enormously comforting. I shake my head remembering my first naïve reaction to his description of the life of the leader—"Why would a principal feel lonely?" Indeed. Jackson's account resonates powerfully with my own experience of administrative loneliness and isolation, and I am grateful to him, an astute envoy who dared to write about this taboo topic. I now know, all too well, what he was talking about.

Jackson writes with insider knowledge. Only someone who has lived leadership could write so eloquently about its nuanced complexities. As administrator of a university lab school for 8 years he had ample opportunity to experience the travails of administrative isolation. He warns the reader of the perplexing nature of this syndrome, a warning he fully knows is insufficient to prepare oneself for its pervasive and potentially debilitating effect. Almost by definition, you need to experience it, but with advance notice you might at least be sensitized enough to recognize its hidden but consuming undercurrent.

> Oddly enough, as I look back on it, one of the chief residues of my own administrative experience is the memory of having felt alone, not in the simple physical sense of being by myself, without companions, but in the deeper psychological sense of being apart from others. I call this odd because, prior to becoming an administrator, I had not anticipated that I would feel that way. Even my familiarity with the lonely-at-the-top stereotype had not prepared me for it . . . in point of fact I had not bothered to think very much at all about how an administrator might feel before I actually found myself in the role. . . . "It began on my first day on the job, triggered without warning." (Jackson, 1977, p. 427)

The element of surprise and feeling unprepared significantly complicates the condition of aloneness that Jackson describes. In fact, the combination of aloneness and not knowing you would feel so alone can have a devastating effect, especially on a new principal who is trying to get an initial footing. In his memoir writing, Jackson goes on to skillfully uncover layers of surprise and bewilderment as he charts the occurrences of these alien experiences in various unexpected settings.

> Isolation, I quickly learned, . . . can and does happen in a crowd. . . . Suddenly I felt visible in a way unfamiliar to me . . . there was something different about this new visibility. First, it seemed to happen almost by magic. It had nothing to do with what I did or did not do. I did not have to earn it, nor could I get rid of it. It was automatically bestowed upon me as a function of my new status. It went with the territory. (Jackson, 1977, p. 427)

THE DARK SECRET ABOUT LEADERSHIP

In one of countless rereads of this article over the years, my eyes were alerted to Jackson's depiction of isolation as "automatically bestowed upon me" and seeming to happen "almost by magic." These phrases promptly dislodged from my memory bank Jonathan's reference to me as a "princess." Now, in full light of Jackson's insight, Jonathan's substitution of "princess" for "principal" illuminated for me an entirely new perspective on the role of the principal. I felt as if a secret, commonly known to wise elders in a leadership role, was being divulged to me for the first time: I am different and apart from those I lead . . . and I am alone.

Once I understood this basic truth, I had a very different perspective on the principalship. I chose not to lead with this chapter because an understanding of aloneness doesn't happen in the beginning of a career, even though its cues and signals are evident from the very start. The more I thought about it, the more I began to realize that Jonathan's conception of a school principal was a compelling metaphor for the isolation and loneliness that Jackson writes about. The image of a princess is of someone who belongs to a distinct and privileged group of people; someone who possesses authority, power, and control of riches; someone whose daily routines and life experiences are very different from the people she rules, and therefore a bit magical. It's not as big a leap as you may think to apply these same images to a school principal. In the eyes of children, and most certainly the teachers, principals belong to a distinct and privileged group that possesses authority, power, and yes, even control of riches (access to budget, privileges, permissions, schedules, classroom assignments, evaluations, tenure and promotions). A principal's daily routines and life experiences are dramatically unlike those of the teachers. The notion of a principal as someone different from the teachers, the axiomatic perception that teachers have of their principals, is key to understanding the role of the school's leader.

THE "MEAN-ING" OF AUTHORITY

The second part of Jonathan's comment to his playmate—"I don't think she's mean—do you?"—exposes a child's interpretation of authority, that it entails meanness, or the disposition for meanness. I often wonder if this interpretation is limited to children, or if it is a generally accepted notion of principals shared by adults as well. People commonly remember their own school principals as crabby or irascible. In adult social situations, most principals (once identified as one) experience an outpouring of remembered stories about "mean elementary school principals" that support the myth. It's uncanny.

What about teachers? Do they consider principals to be mean? The answer to this question has to do with teachers' understanding of authority. Teachers readily acknowledge their principal's authority over them. This is a clear and unchallenged dynamic of the principal–teacher relationship. In fact, teachers are apt to note this relationship at times when it's unnecessary, such as in social situations. I have often been introduced to a teacher's spouse or child as "this is my boss." Although I understood and appreciated the respectful tone that was intended, it felt awkward to me, especially in my early years as principal, when I was much younger than the majority of teachers on the faculty. It startled me a bit; it would never occur to me to introduce a teacher as "this is my employee." And maybe that's the point: I don't need to do that because my authority is unquestioned. So why does the teacher need to emphasize my authority?

The point is that the boss/employee dyad is deeply embedded in the teacher's recognition of you as the principal—a constant reminder of who you are and who they are. In fact, that authority is so personified in "you" that there is no other "you." Their allusion to your authority may be an almost unconscious act to avert any discomforting use by you of that authority. "Please don't hurt me" is probably the implied subtext to "this is my boss."

So, are principals mean? To the extent that principals have authority and could use that authority in punitive ways, it is not an unreasonable presumption. Given that, teachers understandably consider a principal as someone to be wary of. It is this cautious regard, this wariness of how authority will be used, that lurks beneath the foundation of the teacher–principal relationship and may fundamentally define that relationship. This is especially the case in stressful times—during an evaluation observation prior to tenure; when a disgruntled parent registers a complaint about a teacher; during teacher negotiations with the school board—all those times when, for the principal, an easy rapport and unencumbered closeness with teachers are so hoped-for because the authority of the principal must then be exercised and its positive intent can never be entirely assumed to be shared by those affected.

No matter how distasteful it is to think of oneself as being regarded as mean and/or unjust, there will be, nevertheless, the overriding perception that its potentiality validates its reality. To understand how consequential that latent premise can be, you need to appreciate the seriousness with which teachers and others regard the principal's authority. Roland Barth (1990) highlights the consequentiality of the principal's relationship with the teachers as significant to the overall effectiveness of the school. In his long-term experience as a head of school, he points out that the principal–teacher relationship defines the quality of life within that school.

> I have found no characteristic of a good school more pervasive than a healthy principal–teacher relationship—and no characteristic of a troubled school more common than a troubled, embattled administrator–teacher relationship. . . . The relationship between teacher and principal seems to have an extraordinary amplifying effect. It models what all relationships will be. (p. 19)

For the most part, teachers tend to relate to the authority embedded in the role of the principal, not to the person who happens to occupy that role. Whether or not that principal possesses personal qualities that would easily invite friendship beyond the school relationship, it's important for a principal not to lose sight of the "those with authority/those without authority" dynamic that underlies all teacher–principal interactions.

Thus, in fairy tales, there are mean princesses and there are kind princesses. The same is true of principals in schools. As for all human beings, of course, both potentials exist. But the very nature of having authority exacerbates the ever-present danger that the "mean potential" will be realized.

Coupling the image of a princess with the notion of being mean completes the school administrator's identity myth: a person who has authority; power over people who depend on her for that authority; control over many decisions directly affecting the welfare of those he or she leads; and who is presumed to be at best potentially mean and at worst decidedly mean. So, do you want this job? Sure you do. But wait—there's more.

THOSE WHO LED BEFORE YOU

Your leadership as a principal does not occur in a vacuum. It has a particular setting, a set of expectations, and a lineage of leadership, that is, those who came before you. All are defining features that will have an impact on your success as a principal. Also, the physical setting of your school matters. Are you in a small suburban district where everyone is known to each other and business is easily transacted? Or are you in a large urban school district where issues easily achieve a larger political status and the size of a school's faculty and staff can frustrate the possibility of being known and complicate much-needed communication? What are the expectations of you as you assume your leadership? Are there crisis-level concerns awaiting your immediate action? Or is the climate of your school quietly moving along (maybe too quietly), so that any action on your part would be disturbing to the community?

What about the principal(s) who preceded you? Are you the next of a long line of short-term principals? And why is that? Or are you following the long tenure of a much beloved (or not beloved!) principal? Or are you the one who follows the tyrant who was there only briefly?

All of these contextual matters will have an effect on the pace and rhythm of your leadership and your relationship with the teachers and staff. The combination of all the possible contextual variables yields enormously different principal job descriptions. The principal of an urban school of 4,000 students may not view her job as being the same as her colleague-principal in a remote rural school populated by 200 students.

Still, regardless of the specifics of the context, the fundamental reality of leadership remains unchanged—you have authority over others, and therefore you will make decisions that affect a great many people and that will inevitably yield both positive and negative outcomes in their estimation. You should not be surprised that your decisions and actions may be misperceived by others, leading them to regard you in ways you did not intend. In the end, the principal's desk is where the buck stops, and the cost of that buck may be very high in the sense of isolation you are likely to experience at various times during your tenure as principal, an isolation caused by any number of suspicions, resentments, disappointments, or fears of you just because of your "princess" status. But take heart. You are just as likely to find that such feelings are balanced by many of gratitude, admiration, affection and even sometimes, though rarely, an understanding of your plight.

DECISIONS, DECISIONS, DECISIONS

Decision-making is at the core of the principal's job. Principals make unbelievable numbers of decisions. It has been estimated that within a single hour principals are likely to engage in as many as 50 to 60 separate interactions with students, parents, custodians, and teachers—many of these exchanges requiring a decision to be made (Peterson, 2001, pp. 1–2).

Jackson points to decision-making as one of the many sources of aloneness experienced by the school administrator. Although he does not consider the majority of decisions made by school leaders to be particularly momentous (and he is correct on that point), still, even mundane decisions have a cost factor: "The infrequency of big decisions, however, does not diminish their discomfort when they do occur. At such moments the feeling of aloneness intensifies" (Jackson, 1977, pp. 428–429).

What is it about decision-making that induces feelings of aloneness? Is it the weight of the responsibility? Or, possibly, having to live with the outcome of these decisions both on you and those affected by them? In my experience it is surprisingly seldom, if ever, the outcome of any particular decision. Rather, it inevitably winds its way back to that larger issue of authority, the authority that has been bestowed upon you to make that decision. Each time you activate your authority you demonstrate that you reside in a professional space different from—separate from—those you lead. That is how authority intensifies your feelings of aloneness. It highlights your supervisory responsibilities, and the separateness that is required in the fulfillment of those responsibilities.

Your authority is most clearly manifested by the prerogative—the necessity—to make decisions. Each decision you make reveals your values, your thinking, your sensitivities, your philosophy. Your decisions display, for all to see, who you are as a person, a professional, and a leader. You will become known, and certainly remembered, largely by your decisions, as all leaders in all contexts, in all cultures, must be. You cannot escape the decision-making requirement of your position and its consequences.

However, it is possible to confront it in ways that signal to others that you are experiencing either comfort or discomfort with your responsibility. Avoiding decisions, or showing reticence to make decisions, or depending on others to make your decisions for you, are indications that you are uncomfortable with leadership—that you are ill fitted to the acceptance of and requirements for that role. And you will be judged accordingly.

Alternatively, making too many decisions that you don't need to make, thereby freezing others out of their appropriate responsibilities for decision-making, is likely to have the opposite effect, signifying that your leadership is inflated and that you may be abusing it by requiring sole ownership of all decisions. A wise school leader seeks the right balance in authority, that is, knowing when to make a decision and encouraging and enabling others to make decisions that create much-desired multiple layers of shared leadership.

"I'VE DECIDED THAT . . ."

As a beginning principal you may coast by for a time without having to make any noticeable decisions that create ripples in the smooth pond of your school's life. But sooner or later you will have to make that first substantive decision that will inevitably cause some controversy. It can be a decision small in scope (or so you think!). For example, as discussed in Chapter 4, you may change the format of the faculty meeting to eliminate time-consuming announcements so more time can be devoted to the topic selected by the teachers. That sounds so simple. Clearly it wasn't.

Or it may be a significant decision: You decide not to rehire a teacher for the next school year because you lack confidence in her judgment. That sounds difficult. And it is. A decision that consequential will have obvious effects. You are convinced of its unfortunate but required validity. The effects it causes and their consequences for you, however, will not be entirely because you made a hard decision (although those who strongly disagree with it are sure to be deeply affected), but will also reflect matters such as how you carried out that decision, i.e., the timing, sequence, consideration of others' feelings about the decision, the announcement of the decision, and the aftermath of the decision.

Get ready to experience some interpersonal discomfort while the teachers are reviewing your decision and deciding its effect, if any, upon them. They have been anxiously awaiting this initial flexing of your authority muscle—this first glimpse of who you are underneath all the surface of your pleasant-seeming, reasonable-seeming persona. Their discussions will be conducted in hallways, over coffee, in the teachers' lounge, and during drives to and from school, well out of your view and earshot. Still, you'll be viscerally aware of their deliberations and their subtle retreat into that protected space between the leader and the led that defines the boundary of your relationship with them. From that vantage point you are under surveillance while the teachers incorporate your decision into their concept of "who you really are."

It is at this juncture that a myriad of motivations may be attributed to you, some or many not remotely accurate. You'll be puzzled to hear rumors of the rationale for your decision. For example, "You didn't rehire that teacher because you have a friend you've arranged with to replace her." (Huh? I didn't rehire her because I didn't think she was a good teacher. Hire a friend? I never even met the replacement teacher before the interview.)

You'll feel the effect of this first hiccup in your relationship with the teachers. How could this decision—this good decision—eject you out of the community of collegial friendship and caring of the teachers? You feel the teachers have withdrawn from the easy companionship you've come to rely on these past weeks or months. Have you deceived yourself into thinking you can rely on a carefree, uncomplicated relationship with the teachers? Yes, most likely, you have indeed deceived yourself. Here are some basic leadership truths to remember:

- Decision-making causes a sudden, often powerful intrusion into your consciousness of something previously unglimpsed—that leadership entails a separation from the led.
- That "good decision," whatever it was, did not eject you out of the community of collegial friendship and caring of the teachers. You were never part of that community to begin with! The teachers always knew this and now you do, too.
- You didn't do anything wrong. You did something that had to be done for a higher, more significant purpose than protecting the current perception of harmony among your staff. Such higher purposes are what you must serve if your leadership is to be ultimately positive. You also have the responsibility to educate your staff as to the need for sometimes difficult decisions that simply must be made in aid of recognizing impediments to and positive contributions toward the overall success of the school's mission. And you are the one who must make those decisions, despite the inevitable separation that will be evidenced, at least for a while, by your acceptance of your leadership responsibility.

The agony of leadership is just now being realized. You are now initiated into your true community, which is not with your staff, much as you desire it to be and fantasized that it was. It is with other administrators—those, like you, who have authority and must live with the responsibilities and consequences of having it. (By the way, in your building, unless you have an assistant, the membership in that community is likely to be just one. You.) You have joined a new fraternity, that of leaders. And you will find, among them, soulmates who will identify deeply with your role and support you in difficult times.

CONFIDENTIAL INFORMATION AND PRINCIPAL DEMEANOR

As if all of this up-close examination of the realities of authority isn't enough, there are still more layers of burden that accompany it. You must be mindful of how you cope with your own leadership and how you handle the many ways your leadership is perceived by others. Teachers don't really know who you are personally despite their frequent need to share sensitive and confidential information with you about their lives or the lives of their colleagues, with full trust in you to protect that confidentiality and little if any comprehension of the often conflicted positions that thrusts you into.

We've already noted that as principal, you'll have intense feelings of aloneness; you'll often be misunderstood; your trustworthiness will be doubted; you'll have motivations attributed to you that you don't even recognize. Still, in the midst of all this it is expected that you will maintain a grounded and predictable demeanor of calmness and even-temperedness.

Principals need to be vigilant about the constancy of their demeanor. Absence of a greeting due to being momentarily distracted, a preoccupation with other events in your life, a period of heightened frenzy due to too many deadlines and an overly filled schedule, can so easily unleash a series of hallway comments indicating teachers' awareness of a different rhythm. "What's up with her?" "Is she upset with me?" "Did I say something?" Principals come to know that the emotional barometric pressure in the building depends largely on them. If I'm calm, they are calm.

I was interested to learn, regrettably only recently, that there's a physiological reason for that. It's referred to as an open loop.

> An open loop system depends largely on external sources to manage itself. In other words, we rely on connections with other people for our own emotional stability . . . the continual interplay of limbic open loops among members of a group creates a kind of emotional soup, with everyone adding his or her own flavor to the mix. But it is the leader who adds the strongest seasoning. Why? Because of that enduring reality of business: everyone watches the boss. People take their emotional cues from the top. (Goleman, 2004, pp. 6–7.)

The perception of how things are going in a building largely determines the reality of how things are going in the building. Principals know that all eyes are on them all the time. People are taking their emotional cues from us, so a centered, friendly, positive public demeanor is required to help others define their own demeanor and achieve that desired state of natural equilibrium.

HEALING ALONENESS THROUGH COMMUNITY: ANOTHER DEMAND OF LEADERSHIP

Administrative aloneness is not something to be solved—it's to be acknowledged and talked about openly in administrative circles and also with teachers, even though their understanding of and empathy with the issues, absent living the principal's life, will be somewhat limited.

There are many topics not talked about in schools. The irony is that there would be little disagreement among principals or teachers about which topics are "too hot to handle": a particular teacher's troublesome ways of relating to colleagues; another teacher who, while a friend to many, is not performing satisfactorily as a professional; recent heated conversations about teacher contract negotiations; the sometimes uneasy working relationship between classroom teachers, special subject teachers, and special education teachers; the working relationship between paraprofessionals and classroom teachers; the hierarchy of presumed authority on a grade-level team. We need to add "administrative aloneness and isolation" to that list of topics that are subtitled, "Yes, we know it's there, but we just don't want to get into it; it's too threatening, too uncomfortable, too embarrassing, too revealing of my (our) imperfections."

It's important that school leaders realize that they're not imagining that distance—that emargination from the teachers. It's real. When you have a context in which to understand it, it makes a lot of sense. This real aspect of the principalship needs to be talked about openly. To name it is a powerful act of control. To dismiss it as "Oh it's just part of the job" doesn't do it justice. It's important enough to be understood. And that requires a community in which you are safe to reveal and explore its dilemmas.

Many years ago in our district the administrators would go through a process we referred to as a Building Audit. At our regularly scheduled weekly meetings each administrator would take a turn to present their school to their principal colleagues. Other administrators (curriculum, pupil services, business manager) would also present their "jobs" at one of these meetings. With no predetermined format—rather, an evolution of a format that depicted each administrator's particular stage of leadership—we each talked openly about our building, a state-of-the union address of sorts. Our reports to one another were filled with statistics and demographic information, descriptions of good instructional programs, current issues we were facing, and goals we were hoping to achieve.

Principals are accustomed to talking with parent groups or local newspaper interviewers about the state of their building—recent programs for our parent organization that we're proud of, our goals for the year, and so forth. These audits were different. The audience was our administrative colleagues, those who deeply shared our understandings of the special life that school leaders live. Within the safety and confines of our administrative team, we talked about what we weren't proud of, what challenged us as principals. We talked openly about instances of our own poor judgment and sought counsel from one another about how best to handle a similar situation in the future. We talked about what words to use in telling a teacher that their performance lacked adherence to a standard; the persistent tensions in our buildings; an intense parental dialogue requiring a different approach than one regrettably already embarked on. We talked about the many problem-solving needs that required a resolution we could not yet envision. And we shared our feelings of the bubble of separateness in which our work placed us, knowing that here, thankfully, we would be understood, supported, and respected for our attempts to cope, as professionals, with the challenges to our selfhood that our leadership responsibilities presented.

These kinds of conversations are enormously helpful in reenergizing school leaders as they confront the daily challenges of leadership. Whether or not you resolve the issue, the act of talking about it brings immediate relief and unearths problem-solving possibilities you may not be able to imagine by yourself.

On the eve of retirement, I, like many before me, experience the wisdom that only long service can bring. It is my deep wish that school leaders will find the need and the time to talk openly about administrative aloneness and, by doing so, to lighten the heavy burden that its secrecy carries.

GETTING BACK TO KINDERGARTEN

So, where were we? Visiting kindergarten—enjoying the pure and sincere invitation to join children in their play, to know these children well, to create an environment that is safe, to have a good teacher in place who will create happy memories for them. And for you, the principal, to quietly make that all happen.

And if Jonathan is still there and he calls you princess (or prince) instead of principal, I suggest you smile and reflect on the wisdom that only children can provide. Learn the precious lesson that he has offered to you about the paradox of being a successful school principal: you will spend your days exercising authority, being in many ways a trusted colleague and friend, but always, nevertheless, living the leadership life of a separate reality from all who are not playing your role. And remember, your playing that leadership role successfully is perhaps the single most influential factor in creating a good school.

LEADERSHIP LESSONS

- A complex circumstance of leadership is the having of authority that often leads to feelings of aloneness and isolation.
- As a principal, your authority is most clearly demonstrated by the prerogative—the necessity—to make decisions.
- Leadership entails a separation from the led.
- Principals need to be vigilant about the constancy of their demeanor. Principals come to know that the emotional barometric pressure in the building depends largely on them.
- School leaders need time to talk openly about administrative aloneness with others in such positions and, by doing so, to lighten the heavy burden that its secrecy carries.

Clarifying Episode:
The Reception for Retirees

Our small school district has a strong sense of history and a number of rituals and traditions that define us. One of many charming traditions we maintain is an end-of-year reception for that year's and previous retirees, hosted by the members of our Board of Education. The purpose is for present and former staff to come together to celebrate the school year just now ending and to honor and recognize our retirees as they come to the close of their careers. The attendance of those teachers already retired adds credence to our respect for and wish to continue in the path of the history of our schools.

I remember attending my first reception as a beginning principal. Like any newcomer, I noted the room's arrangement and tried to make sense of the event and especially, absent any specific information to guide me, where I should be standing. I noticed that current teachers and staff gathered in the center of the room and those I did not yet recognize, that is, already retired teachers, gathered in concentric outer circles, the more recently retired closer to the center still somewhat connected to the now, and the more long-term retired teachers farther away from the center, watching the busyness and frenetic conversations of those still teaching. The older retirees looked on from the sides to see what's become of our school and our district. They evaluated the look of the group, its youth, its energy, its level of commitment to values of long ago—their own values.

As a brand-new principal I placed myself in the center of the room, confident that my place was there, in the now. I chatted frenetically with the teachers and administrators I knew. As names and faces of the retired teachers were pointed out to me, I assumed the statesmanlike role of a principal. I graciously went about the room to greet my elders, to acknowledge their contributions, to link their gifts to present practice, to reassure them "you're not forgotten." And then I promptly returned to the center, the place where it was happening. I was new and one who would make things happen.

Last spring, I journeyed to the outer circle with eyes opened to my new future. I was greeted warmly and knowingly by those who knew I would soon join their ranks. Feeling as if I were in one of those movies where you are greeted to the "life beyond," I dwelled longer in the outer circle with greatly increased interest in these former teachers' knowledge and the good advice that they were able to give. And then I stepped back into that "happening circle"—one last time.

9

Imagine Not Being a Principal: Passing the Baton

This chapter is intended for career principals and retiring principals. One of the many ironies of being a long term principal is that once you've endured your struggles and put your mark on your school it's probably time to go. With a reasonable degree of humility, you look back on your career and review the highlights and some inescapable "lowlights" as well. Leaving a school is not an easy task. With luck, you are able to have enough warning to carefully and thoughtfully ready everyone—including yourself—for the transition. This inevitable occurrence of one's end of career calls for qualities of leadership to avoid causing feelings of abandonment and to elevate a sense of renewal for the school, community, and oneself.

D EAR COLLEAGUES,

I am concluding this book with a letter to you, my colleagues—principals already in the schools for some years. Although we may not have met, we know one another well. We all belong to that vast fraternity of leaders all over the world who know the "secret handshake" and readily support one another in countless ways. No matter where our school is located, its size of enrollment, or its type of community, we have relied on one another. In absence of possibly ever having been in the same room together, we, the schools' leaders, all think the same thoughts, experience the same frustrations, and devote ourselves to our absurd collection of duties and responsibilities known by that simple label—principal.

At some point, believe it or not, you will leave your principalship. The circumstances, context, and details vary for each of us. I am retiring after

having a fulfilling career. I'm not ambivalent about leaving, but, nevertheless, leaving is enormously difficult for me. I have spent the last two decades
of my life worrying, planning, coping, being responsible for, and generally
living my life always mindful of my school. I have been the boss, and now I
won't be that any longer.

We all know that the life of a school doesn't stand still while we principals struggle with our personal feelings about these natural transitions. Our
leadership skills—the best of them—are needed to the very end. That being
so, it made sense to me to use the occasion of my leaving as a final leadership project: how best to mentor the principal who will replace me. I realize
that my knowing and having the opportunity to work with my successor may
be considered an unusual circumstance. Certainly, the idea of a principal
leaving a school and a new principal beginning in that leadership role is
unremarkable, possibly too unremarkable. And that's my point. I've been
thinking a lot about mentoring in general and the issues raised in the national media about "who wants this principal job?" We know better than
anyone that there's good reason for asking that question. Still, for many of
us, we're deeply appreciative of having had the opportunity to serve in this
leadership role. The question remains, however: who will take our place and,
of significant concern, who will mentor them?

We all lament the fact that we didn't have more and better direction at
the beginnings of our career. As veteran principals, we've learned a lot of
hard-earned lessons about leadership. As we approach the close of our career, we consider how best to hand down that wisdom to those of our suc-
cessors who are accepting their first principalship or are preparing themselves
to do so. Their success will be enhanced immeasurably by expert mentoring
at that tender time in their professional lives. So we need to think back to
the beginnings of our own careers as principals—to get ourselves into that
mind-set so we can regain an appreciation of newness to leadership and be
generous, but prudent, with our advice to them.

I'd like to share some thoughts with you about my ending process and
my role in facilitating the transition to the new leadership of my school, which
I hope you will find helpful at that point in your career. I've structured this
letter using the outline of this book, so that we could reflect together on whether
the dimensions of leadership that I've selected to highlight in it are useful as
guidelines for preparing those who will carry on our efforts. Let's see if it works.

MENTORING A PRINCIPAL WHO IS IMAGINING
WHAT IT WILL BE LIKE

As I considered the complexity of the mentoring task, I quickly realized that
I could not be the sole source of information and support for my successor.

Ongoing successful mentoring of a new principal would require the active involvement of all the stakeholders. My final leadership project, not unexpectedly, would have to be far wider in scope than I had first realized. What to do? In order to ready all those appropriately to be involved in this project, I needed to mentor multiple mentors, in effect, the entire school—teachers, children, parents, and community, all of whom would wish to contribute their perspective to the new leader. That would be a really big project. So I needed to begin before the new principal was selected.

I chose letter-writing as one vehicle to acknowledge the multiple audiences and layers of information involved in readying the school for new leadership. For me, letters most closely approximate the personal, conversational tone that invites involvement and builds a foundation for future focused discussion. In order to get myself into that reflective mind-set, I thought back to my first years as principal, and long before that time, to my childhood dreams. I grew up in the 1950s, and I was one of those kids who loved paint-by-number kits. Whether it was colored pencils or a tray of nicely organized watercolors, I would spend endless hours matching the numbered spaces with the correct pencil or paint until the preplanned image of a seascape or a farm scene emerged. The tidiness of the experience and absence of risk were attractive conditions for me. Painting by numbers satisfied the compliant and solitary parts of my personality, and my strong need for structure. I used to think that those personality characteristics would follow me into adulthood and my choice of career. I was wrong. I never imagined that I would become a school principal, a career that called upon an entirely different set of dispositions than those I had enjoyed as a child.

As a beginning elementary school principal I, like you no doubt, quickly realized there was no lovely packaged set of pencils and a preplanned template, that is, the sole tools I would need to be successful. I needed to develop comfort with open-ended and unpredictable rhythms to my workdays. Schools are, in some ways, rule-bound, structured organizations; however, as a beginning principal, I confronted an almost entirely clean canvas when I embarked on that leadership path. Although I longed for the tidiness and correctness of a paint-by-number tableau, I was charged, instead, with creating a work of art out of the conditions, personalities, and needs that existed when I took the helm. Instead of correctly numbered pencils, my work tools were those unchangeables of leadership—responsibility, my life experiences and temperament, my judgment, courage, and a guiding vision of a good school. These tools shaped my authority as a principal and were embedded in the many decisions I made, which in turn became known and recognized as the image of my leadership. Without knowing anything about the true nature of the job, I recalled that simple pledge I made to myself when I was first appointed—to listen and to be a good principal.

We will all have different important lessons to pass on to our less experienced colleagues. For me, I remembered my own awkward way of calling up each teacher on that rotary-dial telephone, and I considered what would be a better way for my successor to get to know these teachers and for my staff to introduce themselves. Not surprisingly, the idea of a letter seemed appropriate to me. I invited each staff member to write a letter to the new principal—yet to be named. My letter to the teachers is shown in Figure 9.1.

This would provide the teachers and staff with an opportunity to introduce and reveal themselves in a manner of their own choosing, rather than relying on the exchange of information between the two principals or on the new principal studying their personnel files.

COMBINING LEADERSHIP WITH MANAGEMENT

Don't be surprised to discover that ending your career as principal and leaving a school is filled with an inordinate number of details. Your management skills will be put to full use. Remember to stay the course and absorb those details within the larger leadership mission of readying the staff, parents, and students for the transition to a new principal and their role in helping to make that person successful.

If you've been principal of your building for a long period, you realize the difficulties involved in announcing your leaving. The announcement itself needs to be timed and sequenced well to coincide with the different stakeholders' need to know and the timeline for the recruitment process. I chose the end of the prior year—late May—that time of the year when most of us are running on adrenaline. For the teachers and staff, late May is the time of year when an announcement of leaving can be incorporated into other endings. Teachers hear this news and know it's not happening right now. They go about the busyness of end-of-year activities and have a long summer and the following year to incorporate that announcement into their lives.

Our staff is small, and so a face-to-face announcement at a faculty meeting was the appropriate way for me to notify them of my plans to retire. It took me some weeks of anxious preparation and I actually practiced the exact wording in order to gather the courage to make my announcement. I scheduled a meeting with the leaders of our parent organization immediately following the faculty meeting announcement. Parents appreciate being in the know about a significant change in their school's staffing as early as possible. I had prepared a letter to parents—shown in Figure 9.2—that went into the mail that afternoon.

FIGURE 9.1. Letter to Staff—Inviting Letters to New Principal

September 2004

Dear Faculty,

   As I think about transitioning you to a new administrator, it occurs to me that many principals approach the topic of goals in different ways than I do. I want to ready you for that change so that you don't have lots that's new at the same time.
   Another important goal I have is for you to have an authentic vehicle for your principal to know you—as you want to be known. Think for a moment about how you come to know your new students for the year. Many of you are hesitant to read a child's file lest it influence your initial impressions. Portfolios are available to you, but best shown to you by the child. And where's the time for that? But you do read parent letters about the child and I think most of you find these letters very helpful in gaining a beginning sense of each student and family.
   It's not too different for a new principal. As I've often told you, you are my classroom. A new principal has those same reservations about reading files and yet wants to get to know you. How wonderful and appropriate it would be for your new principal to have a brief letter from you about you.
   In aid of all of these goals, I'm going to ask you to submit a one-page REFLECTION. A very rough outline of your REFLECTION might include this information:

   • Who are you? (any autobiographical information; how long
      you've been at CI; grades/subjects taught, etc.)

   • I am confident of my ability to . . .

   • Challenges for me include . . .

   • At this stage in my career, I'm interested in . . .

   This is by NO MEANS the only way to prepare this document. A one-page (yes, it can be longer only if you'd like and feel compelled) reflection, and accompanying photo would be great. I envision it as a possible letter to your new principal OR in a format that you imagine.
   Let me know if you'd like to chat about this project.

   Thanks,
   B.

FIGURE 9.2. Letter to Parents—Retirement Announcement

May 2004

Dear Parents,

    Twenty years ago I came to Winnetka as principal of Crow Island School. I'm not exaggerating when I tell you I have eagerly anticipated coming to school every day of these past two decades. I consider myself very fortunate to have served in this important post. However, the inevitable question of when to conclude my principalship has occupied my thoughts. After considerable reflection I have decided to bring closure to this aspect of my career at the end of the next school year in June 2005.

    I have many interests I'd like to explore in my remaining years of professional involvement. In order to do so, I've come to the conclusion that I need to take that big, brave first step of committing to a yet to be defined next career path. I plan to consider several education-related interests that I have already started to pursue, such as professional writing, university teaching, consulting with architects about the process of designing new schools, working with teachers and principals about the best uses of student portfolios, and other possibilities still to be imagined.

    I want you to know about my decision now so that we are all well prepared for a smooth transition to new leadership for Crow Island. The members of the school board and Superintendent Becky van der Bogert are preparing a process that will include your input. You'll be hearing more about that process over the coming months.

    As for now, it's very much business as usual. The teachers and I are busily engaged as we bring the current school year to a successful close and plan for the coming year. I will have next year's list of teacher assignments for you in the *Bulletin* at the end of the month.

    Please know that I so appreciate all you do to support our school. We couldn't do our work without your help and encouragement.

All best wishes for a relaxing summer,

Elizabeth A. Hebert
Principal

A SCHOOL'S HISTORY, TRADITIONS, AND RITUALS

During the final year, veteran principals confront the sometimes enormous accumulation of files and projects gathered over the course of their tenure. It's natural to feel overwhelmed by this history—particularly the task of organizing it, and deciding how best to communicate where we've been as

a school over these past years. It occurred to me at that exasperated moment that I wasn't communicating that history only to a new principal.
Many of the parents and teachers newer to the school were understandably not aware of significant chunks of our school's history, the background
information, the way we do some things the way we do and the why we do
them. I began to think of some way of documenting the school's history
for a larger audience as well as providing much-needed information to the
new principal.

With that spirit and goal in mind, I began to compose letters to the new
principal, like the one shown in Figure 9.3, each with a distinct theme, and
I incorporated some of them into our school's weekly *Bulletin* to parents.

Here is the *introduction* to that series of letters.

> Dear New Principal of Crow Island,
>
> Welcome! This is the first of a series of letters I plan to write to
> you. My purposes are several. I feel the obligation to provide guid-
> ance to you and to share some history of the school and where we've
> been these last two decades. I plan to share some of these letters in
> our weekly newsletter to the parents, the *Bulletin*. Many of our
> parents are new to Crow Island and these letters give me an authentic
> vehicle to inform them of our school's history and ways of being.
> Please accept these reflections from your predecessor in the collegial
> spirit they are offered.

As you pass the baton, you'll be anxious to reinforce the many rituals
and traditions that have made your school so special to you and everyone
else who experienced it. The comfort of the school's ceremonies can be a
powerful mechanism to unify the community in a stressful year.

One test of the rituals and traditions of a school is to see if they are
sufficient and sturdy enough to carry us through times of joy, sorrow, and
transition. I called upon many of our traditions as vehicles to say goodbye
and to remind us of our strength and resilience as a community. I was heart-
ened to discover that, true to the defining role of traditions, they were able
to serve as familiar placeholders for the many emotions and anxieties we were
all experiencing in our final year together. The collection of the year's traditions served as a gradual crescendo from fall through spring. The beginning
of the year welcome assembly; our Halloween Walk; the parent/teacher party
in January, the springtime revving up of ceremonies that signal the approach-
ing end of the school year; Spring Sing assemblies; end-of-year letters to staff,
parents, and students; all served a purpose in demonstrating that our school
life would continue safely as we welcomed the new leader to share in it, and
perhaps to enhance it in original ways.

FIGURE 9.3. Letter to New Principal

FROM BETH HEBERT: A new occasional column in the *Bulletin* this year—
My Letters to the New Principal. Though the interview process for the new
principal of Crow Island is just starting, it's not too soon to begin sharing
some of my reflections on the principalship with the Crow Island community
and my successor:

Dear New Principal of Crow Island,

This is the second in a series of letters I plan to write to you. As I said in
my first letter, my purposes are several. As a veteran principal of 21 years, I
feel the obligation of providing guidance to you and sharing some history of
the school and where we've been these last two decades. I plan to share some
(not all!) of these letters in our weekly newsletter to the parents, the
Bulletin. Many of our parents are new to Crow Island and these letters give
me an authentic vehicle to inform them of our school's history and ways of
being. Please accept these reflections from your predecessor in the collegial
spirit they are offered. I call this letter **"Crow Island School—A National
Landmark."**

I will address you as "New Principal of Crow Island School," even after
your name is known to us. My hope is that you feel the full impact of your
new position. You are not only a principal—you are the principal of Crow
Island School—"the best school ever made!" These words come from Helen
Long's (student in the '60s) lyrics to our school song. Some will say these
simple words refer to the architecture but truly Helen was depicting a spirit—
now yours to maintain.

Crow Island School is now 64 years old and has been widely recognized
for its architectural significance. In 1971, the American Institute of Architects
(AIA) selected Crow Island School for their prestigious 25-Year-Award, an
award also given to Rockefeller Center in New York, among other buildings.
In 1990, the U.S. Department of the Interior designated Crow Island as a
National Historic Landmark. Thousands of students have experienced this
humane surrounding which was built to demonstrate architecturally the
respect and regard its planners held for childhood as a period of life in which
learning, and the joy it affords, is a central goal. This thoughtfully designed
environment has succeeded in responding to the educational needs of
successive generations of children through all the many changes that have
occurred since 1940, because the fundamental design philosophy of child
development as a personal quest has remained valid over time.

In addition to your many responsibilities as instructional leader, support
professional to teachers, children, and parents; innovator and mentor of good
ideas; problem-solver, personnel expert, facility manager, and traffic manager

FIGURE 9.3. (continued)

(oh, that's another long letter!), you have another job. The school you are now principal of just happens to be a National Historic Landmark and so you will now serve as chief steward of your building facility. Crow Island School is an important building in the eyes of the world so this aspect of your principalship requires special attention.

On any given day busloads of architects may surprise you as they graciously appear in the foyer wanting to take even a brief glimpse of an "architectural mecca." Take some time to watch them observing the building and you'll learn a lot. Architects gaze at the open space of the foyer and they shake their heads in amazement at the many walls of windows. "1940, did you say? . . . it was built in 1940?" they ask incredulously. Many of these architects know a lot about Crow Island. Still, they marvel at its many wonderful features. They run their hands across the ponderosa pine walls—surfaces that have been stapled into to display children's work for over six decades. They measure the expansive width of hallways by counting floor tiles; they notice the lowered ceilings; they stand in awe of our auditorium and the rows of benches becoming smaller and smaller as they walk toward the stage. They smile as they notice the height of door handles and light switches. Architects also watch the children—how the children use the building—how they easily enter classroom doors thoughtfully announced in primary colors; how the children lean against a brick-walled hallway protected by three simple wooden strips. These architects note a rugtime gathering of children framed by a skylight overhead and they marvel at the openness of the surroundings and the wooded setting.

As the school's principal I have toured many of these visiting architects over the years and I notice what they look at and record in their sketchbooks. But as an educator, I observe children carefully, and I notice for myself the powerful effect of well designed space on children—their behavior—their learning—their attitudes and dispositions. And it holds true as I observe the teachers and staff as well. When a building is made right—it makes a difference in our lives.

Another of your many responsibilities as principal is to seize opportunities for promoting the good work of the school and informing a larger public about your school's significance. The celebration of Crow Island School's 50th Anniversary in the fall of 1990 provided a unique opportunity to involve teachers, parents, and community members in one of those larger-than-life projects that examined the history of Crow Island, nurtured the ever-present sense of pride we have in our school, and reminded all of us about the powerful connection between learning and the design of a school in which that learning happens.

You'll find lots of files and mention of this grand celebration, but here's a brief summary of what we did: In 1987 a small group of teachers, parents, architects and community members convened to talk about how we might celebrate the 50th anniversary of Crow Island at that time, three years away.

FIGURE 9.3. (continued)

We gathered ideas and designated committees for each area of interest that we listed: Alumni Search, Docent Training Program, Homecoming Weekend & Celebration Event, Restoration, Publicity, Crow Island Archive, National Landmark Status Application, Education/Architecture Conference. We set about our work as separate committees and then came together every few months to inform each other of our progress and next steps. Committees grew in number and so did our ideas and our momentum. Collecting memories of over two thousand Crow Island alums, designation as a National Historic Landmark, organizing a docent training program still running to this day, and hosting a 1st International Conference for Educators and Architects supported by the National Endowment for the Arts, the Graham Foundation, the New York Times Education Fund and the Consulate of Finland were just a few of the many events and projects that unleashed the autonomous spirit and capabilities of many people. It was, indeed, a memorable time in Crow Island's history.

Celebration is an important component of community. A school's principal is expected to encourage and nurture occasions for the values of the school community to be affirmed and honored. Another opportunity for celebrating Crow Island presented itself last spring. Just outside the main office on the north wall of the hallway, you'll see a museum-quality exhibit entitled "Philosophy in Brick." Take some time to study this exhibit and you'll have completed a course in the history of Crow Island School. Three Crow Island teachers, Eva Tarini, Mary Mumbrue, and Bliss Tobin, in addition to their teaching responsibilities, collaborated over a five-year period in an extensive research into the history of our school. These teachers, profoundly influenced by the powerful intent of Crow Island school and inspired by their caring commitment to being part of a strong professional community, devoted themselves to concretizing a passionate belief into this memorable exhibit for the benefit of children, colleagues and community for years to come. Last March our PTA hosted a celebratory opening of this exhibit, a memorable event. Needless to say, I am enormously proud of these colleagues, but I must say it's the kind of experience I've come to know as emblematic of the strong professional culture in the Winnetka Public Schools.

There are few schools, if any, as well known, as often photographed, or as well designed as Crow Island. There are thousands of books, articles, and other media that include some piece of Crow Island history. We've managed to collect quite a bit of the Crow Island literature in our archive. Take some time to learn about your school. I sincerely hope that you come to love and cherish this building as I have. You are indeed very fortunate to be principal of "the best school ever made."

With my best wishes,
Beth

A NEW CHALLENGE FOR FACULTY MEETINGS

Our twice-monthly faculty meetings served as a major vehicle for readying the staff and myself for the transition to new leadership. At each meeting during my final year I took full advantage of the announcements portion of our meetings. I shared many of the "Clarifying Episodes" found between the chapters of this book. My purposes in doing so were to acknowledge my feelings about leaving and to clarify how a principal thinks, all in anticipation of a new principal's presence. I referred to them as Final Thoughts, and this is how I introduced them:

> This year, in addition to sharing general pieces of news, from time to time I'll include "Final Thoughts"—some things I want to tell you— things you need to know or realize before the close of this year. My remaining time with you is brief, so when I glimpse a context for these "final thoughts" you can be sure I'll grab it, via an announcement at faculty meeting or a memo, or possibly a letter.
>
> As I announced my retirement to you last week, I realized that we are in sync right now—possibly more in sync than we ever have been. That's one of those by-products of leaving. Leadership, specifically authority, has been a complicating circumstance of our relationship. At times, a principal's authority acts as a baffle to your really hearing me. It's part of being a principal. It goes with the job.
>
> So, now, as my authority over you slips away, I have this narrow window of opportunity for us to have good conversations based on a different understanding of our relationship. That old perception can be replaced with unencumbered communication and perspective. I have no agenda other than that I know something—and you need to know it, too.

I wasn't sure how the tone of these reflections would be received by the teachers. I was delighted to discover that they enjoyed them. On more than one occasion when I forgot to sign up to make an announcement at the next faculty meeting, I noted that someone entered my name on the list of announcers with the notation "Final Thoughts" next to it. I underestimated the staff's interest in these episodes, a reminder that sharing vulnerability brings me closer to them.

HIRING A NEW PRINCIPAL: WHAT ARE THE QUESTIONS?

Shortly after the school year began the teachers were involved in the process of interviewing candidates for their new principal. Our superintendent took great care to meet with all of the teachers and staff so that everyone would have an opportunity to provide her with their insights in answer to the implicit concern, *"How do we choose a new leader who will help us be all we can be?"*

We used our faculty meeting time for discussing the most pressing matter for the faculty—how to prepare themselves to participate in the interviewing of candidates. Every one of the teachers had had the experience of being interviewed by a committee of colleagues, and almost all had at one time or another served on a faculty interview committee. The teachers made good use of our school's interview procedures as they began to consider what questions to ask. After examining familiar questions and discussing their relevance to the upcoming interview, the teachers were comforted to learn how much they already knew about the interview process. They were prepared.

READYING THE STUDENTS

My initial energies were focused on the adults—staff members and parents. Now my attentions had to turn to how best to tell the students. A principal's relationship with the students will dictate the most appropriate process for informing them that you are leaving and that the school will have a new principal. For the most part, elementary-age children are appropriately focused on issues pertinent to their own lives. Will we be safe? Will the new principal be nice? Will the rules change? Can we still ride bikes to school? A principal quickly learns of those aspects of school life that the children associate with a principal's authority. Without saying it in words, the students are accustomed to the way their school seems to them, its physical look, and its routines and expectations, as well as the more deeply experienced moral and ethical atmosphere of the school.

In acknowledgment of the varying developmental needs of children from kindergarten to fourth grade, and the fact that it was much too early to talk about it, the staff and I decided not to make any general announcement to the children that prior spring. Still, we were mindful that many parents would share this news. So I suggested to the teachers some language to use as needed and as appropriate when the topic came up in their classrooms. Over the course of a year the children learned about the words *retire* and *retirement* and put their own spin on it. (One fourth-grader announced to me that he was going to "retire from doing homework"—his own private acknowledgment of my leaving, no doubt!)

Truly, one of the most anxiety-producing duties of my leaving was figuring out exactly when I would tell the students personally and what words to use. At a moment when I was mulling that issue, one of my second-grade girls spotted me in the hallway and posed this simple query, "Will you give us something to remember you by?" Gulp! "Yes, of course I will," I assured her. The search for the perfect birthday pencil (my ritual with the students) consumed weeks of my mental energies. Which pencil color? What about the eraser color? And the band—silver or gold? Could they put our school's emblem on it? What message should I include on the pencil? After considerable fretting, the boxes of pencils arrived. During the final week of school I visited each classroom to sit down with each group of children and to distribute the pencils and a letter I wrote to them (Shown in figure 9.4).

WELCOMING A NEW PRINCIPAL

Exercising her insightful leadership, our wise superintendent prepared an extensive and inclusive selection process which, in addition to the faculty and staff at our school, involved collaboration with our parent group and the community. The interview process was completed in the first part of December. The selection of our new principal, already an assistant principal in the school district, was welcomed with great approbation by all of the stakeholders. Due to the early decision and the proximity of her current position, further rich mentoring experiences became possible. I was able to easily include her in my communications to staff, copy her with e-mails, and, overall, provide her with daily annotations of our school's life from January through June. The new principal's visits to the school throughout the spring were enormously helpful to all of us in adjusting to the impending change. In anticipation of these visits, I gave each teacher a copy of a picture of our new principal and suggested they simply put it somewhere in the classroom and, when it seemed appropriate, point it out to the students. In this way, the students were able to recognize the new principal when they saw her in the hallways.

Throughout the spring, my successor attended school events and meetings with staff and parents. There is possibly no way of sufficiently mentoring a new principal colleague about all the nuances and details associated with those highly complex parts of the job, like classroom placement, so it was most helpful that she was able to be with us for the meetings when we organized that all-important first draft of next year's class groupings.

The reality of administrative aloneness so central to the life of a school's leader changes dramatically when the conditions that cause it are in process of being relinquished. Decisions based on the authority of the leader are now quieted. As you enter an "authority-free zone," the causes of the aloneness and isolation begin to dissipate in a rather surreal fashion. While you can alert the new principal to the reality he/she will have to face, of the inevitability of

FIGURE 9.4. Goodbye Letters to Students

June 2005

Dear 1st Graders in _____ Class,

You are coming to the final weeks of 1st grade at Crow Island. You have all worked very hard this year and learned a lot. You are a member of a great class of students, and I have lots of good memories of all of you.

I am still singing the wonderful tunes from your Spring Sing in April, "*Welcome to the Farm.*" I've watched the video of that program over and over again. You really surprised me with that last song, "*Inch by Inch.*" You worked so hard on that program—learning the words to the songs and holding up the artwork and remembering the introductions. WOW!—that was a LOT of work.

I am so proud of all of you: (first names of students in that classroom)!

Many of you have asked me, "Dr. Hebert, what will you do now?" I will be working hard to finish a book I am writing. The title is "*The Boss of the Whole School.*" I thank all the boys and girls at Crow Island for giving me the idea for that title. When I visited your classes when you were in kindergarten, your teacher would often ask you, "Boys and girls, do you know what a principal does?" One or more of you was sure to say, "*She's the boss of the whole school.*" I thought that would be a good title, don't you? When I'm finished with it, I'll come by and show it to you.

I love to write and I think it's important, so I'll be giving each of you one last special birthday pencil. On the side it reads "Happy Birthday . . . always!" I feel honored to have been your principal and I will always keep you in my heart.

With much love,
Dr. Hebert

that separation, the leader will have to discover its force in his/her life. It will have to be experienced personally over time, just as had to be the case with each prior principal. Our mentoring, in this regard, must be honest but also modest. Some things just can't be understood before they are lived through.

A CALL FOR MENTORING

We tend to separate the processes of leaving and beginning. A principal's leaving and the process of seeking and naming the new principal is referred to as the "transition." Once the new principal is on board, we then think of mentoring as giving helpful advice and assistance. In this view, transitioning is focused on the prior principal and mentoring is focused on the new principal. If we consolidate and integrate these functions and focus on the school and its community instead of its past and present leaders, we may reconceive the task of mentoring the school to embark successfully on its next journey. This richer concept of mentoring can open up related conversations and ideas that provide much needed support to everyone involved in that school's life—teachers, children, parents, and community. With mentoring the school as the focus, the principal who is leaving has an opportunity to engage in one of the highest forms of leadership, to thoughtfully and humanely ready the school for new leadership.

In closing, I want to thank you and my many administrative colleagues for the innumerable times you've helped me resolve a problem, given me a good lead on hiring a teacher, or just been there to listen. In doing so you gave me a community of shared experience and understanding that was so precious to my well-being professionally and personally. I have deeply appreciated your advice and counsel over the years. I wish you the very best in all of your life's pursuits.

With cordial good wishes,
Beth Hebert

References

Barth, R. (1980). *Run school run*. Cambridge, MA: Harvard University Press.

Barth, R. (1984). Sandboxes and honeybees. *Education Week, 3*(33), 24.

Barth, R. (1990). *Improving schools from within*. San Francisco: Jossey-Bass.

Crow Island School.—Annual School Improvement Plan: 2004–05. Winnetka, IL: Winnetka Public Schools.

Goleman, D., Boyatzik, R., & McKee, A. (2004). *Primal leadership—Learning to lead with emotional intelligence*. Boston, MA: Harvard Business School Press.

Goodman, J., & Lesnick, H. (2001). *The moral stake in education*. New York: Longman.

Hebert, E. A. (1999). Rugtime for teachers: Reinventing the faculty meeting. *Phi Delta Kappan, 81*(3), 219–222.

Hebert, E. A. (2001). *The power of portfolios*. San Francisco: Jossey-Bass.

Heifetz, R. A., & Linsky, M. (2002). *Leadership on the line: Staying alive through the dangers of leading*. Boston, MA: Harvard Business School Press.

Jackson, P. W. (1977). Lonely at the top: Observations on the genesis of administrative isolation. *School Review, 85*(3), 425–432.

Johnson, S. M., & The Project on the Next Generation of Teachers. (2004). *Finders and keepers—Helping new teachers survive and thrive in our schools*. San Francisco: Jossey-Bass.

Kleiman, C. (2004). Best interview questions. *Chicago Tribune*, October 28, 2004.

Long, H. (1960s). *Good Old Crow Island*. [Crow Island School song, written by Helen when she was a student at Crow Island.] Crow Island School Archive, Winnetka, IL.

Martin, C. (n. d.). Minutes of student council meetings. Crow Island School Archive, Winnetka, IL.

Meier, D. (1996). The big benefits of smallness. *Educational Leadership, 54*(1), 12–15.

Peterson, K. D. (2001). The roar of complexity—A principal's day is built on fragments of tasks and decisions. *Journal of Staff Development, 22*(1), 1–2.

Price, H. B. (2005). Winning hearts & minds. *Education Week, 24*(19), 35.

Schön, D. (1984). *The reflective practitioner: How professionals think in action*. New York: Basic Books.

Sergiovanni, T. (1996). *Leadership for the school house*. San Francisco: Jossey-Bass.

Washburne, C. (1952). *What is progressive education?* New York: The John Day Company.

Washburne, C., & Marland, S. (1963). *Winnetka: The history and significance of an educational experiment.* Englewood Cliffs, NJ: Prentice-Hall.

Winnetka Public Schools. (1981). *Philosophy of the Winnetka Public Schools.* Winnetka, IL: Author

Further Readings

Ackerman, R., Donaldson, G., & van der Bogert, R. (1996). *Making sense as a school leader*. San Francisco: Jossey-Bass.

Ackermann, R., & Maslin-Ostrowski, P. (2002). *The wounded leader*. San Francisco: Jossey-Bass.

Beck, L. G., & Murphy, J. (1993). *Understanding the principalship—Metaphorical themes 1920s–1990s*. New York: Teachers College Press.

Chauncey, C. (Ed.). (2005). *Recruiting, retaining, and supporting highly qualified teachers*. Cambridge, MA: Harvard Education Press.

Coles, R. (1997). *The moral intelligence of children*. New York: Random House.

Corsaro, W. (2003). *We're friends, right?* Washington, DC: Joseph Henry Press.

Cotton, K. (2003). *Principals and student achievement—What the research says*. Alexandria, VA: Association for Supervision and Curriculum Development.

Daresh, J. C. (2001). *What it means to be a principal—Your guide to leadership*. Thousand Oaks, CA: Corwin Press.

Deal, T., & Peterson, K. (1999). *Shaping school culture—The heart of leadership*. San Francisco: Jossey-Bass.

Donaldson, G. (2001). *Cultivating leadership in schools*. New York: Teachers College Press.

Duckworth, E. (1996). *The having of wonderful ideas*. New York: Teachers College Press.

Fullan, M. (1997). *What's worth fighting for in the principalship?* New York: Teachers College Press.

Gardner, H. (1995). *Leading minds—An anatomy of leadership*. New York: Basic Books.

Goodman, S. (1999). The power of listening. *Education Week, 19*(14),35.

Greenspan, S. I. (1993). *Playground politics—Understanding the emotional life of your school-age child*. Reading, MA: Perseus Books.

Hebert, E. A. (1998). Lessons learned about student portfolios. *Phi Delta Kappan, 79*(8), 583–585.

Heller, D. (2004). *Teachers wanted—attracting and retaining good teachers*. Alexandria, VA: Association for Supervision and Curriculum Development.

Jackson, P., Boostrom, R., & Hansen, D. (1993). *The moral life of schools*. San Francisco: Jossey-Bass.

Kriete, R. (2002). *The morning meeting book*. Greenfield, MA: Northeast Foundation for Children.

Levine, A. (2005). *Educating school leaders.* Washington, DC: The Education Schools Project.

Lovely, S. (2004). *Staffing the principalship—Finding, coaching, and mentoring school leaders.* Alexandria, VA: Association for Supervision and Curriculum Development.

Mitgang, L. (2003). "Beyond the pipeline": Getting the principals we need where they are needed most. New York: Wallace Foundation.

Palmer, P. (1998). *The courage to teach—Exploring the inner landscape of a teacher's life.* San Francisco: Jossey-Bass.

Perlow, L. (2003). *When you say yes but mean no—How silencing conflict wrecks relationships and companies and what you can do about it.* New York: Crown Business.

Popp, M. S. (2004). *The man who became a school.* Lanham, MD: Scarecrow Education.

Pristash, S. (2002). *What people think principals do.* Lanham, MD: Scarecrow Press.

Robbins, P., & Alvy, H. (2004). *The new principal's fieldbook—Strategies for success.* Alexandria, VA: Association for Supervision and Curriculum Development.

Schmidt, L. (2002). *Gardening in the minefield—A survival guide for school administrators.* Portsmouth, NH: Heinemann.

Sergiovanni, T. (2000). *The lifeworld of leadership—Creating culture, community, and personal meaning in our schools.* San Francisco: Jossey-Bass.

Sigford, J. L. (2005). *Who said school administration would be fun? Coping with a new emotional and social reality* (2nd ed.). Thousand Oaks, CA: Corwin Press.

Sigsgaard, E. (2005). *Scolding—Why it hurts more than it helps.* New York: Teachers College Press.

Smulyan, L. (2000). *Balancing acts: Women principals at work.* Albany: State University of New York Press.

Stein, S. I., & Gewirtzman, L. (2003). *Principal training on the ground.* Portsmouth, NH: Heinemann.

Surowiecki, J. (2004). *The wisdom of crowds—Why the many are smarter than the few and how collective wisdom shapes business, economies, societies, and nations.* New York: Doubleday.

Tannen, D. (1998). *The argument culture.* New York: Random House.

Thorpe, R. (Ed.). (1995). *The first year as principal—Real world stories from America's principals.* Portsmouth, NH: Heinemann.

Tyack, D. (1999). "What's good in education?" *Education Week, 18*(41).

Washburne, C. (1940). *A living philosophy of education.* New York: John Day.

Wood, C. (1997). *Yardsticks—Children in the classroom ages 4–14.* Greenfield, MA. Northeast Foundation for Children.

Wortman, R. (1996). *Administrators supporting school change.* Portland, ME: Stenhouse Publishers.

Index